I0017700

THE INSANELY EASY GUIDE TO PIXEL 8A

AN EASY TO UNDERSTAND GUIDE TO PIXEL AND ANDROID 14

SCOTT LA COUNTE

RIDICULOUSLY
SIMPLE BOOKS

ANAHEIM, CALIFORNIA

www.RidiculouslySimpleBooks.com

Copyright © 2024 by Scott La Counte.

All rights reserved. No part of this publication may be reproduced, distributed or transmitted in any form or by any means, including photocopying, recording, or other electronic or mechanical methods, without the prior written permission of the publisher, except in the case of brief quotations embodied in critical reviews and certain other noncommercial uses permitted by copyright law.

Limited Liability / Disclaimer of Warranty. While best efforts have been used in preparing this book, the author and publishers make no representations or warranties of any kind and assume no liabilities of any kind with respect to accuracy or completeness of the content and specifically the author nor publisher shall be held liable or responsible to any person or entity with respect to any loss or incidental r consequential damages caused or alleged to have been caused, directly, or indirectly without limitations, by the information or programs contained herein. Furthermore, readers should be aware that the Internet sites listed in this work may have changed or disappeared. This work is sold with the understanding that the advice inside may not be suitable in every situation.

Trademarks. Where trademarks are used in this book this infers no endorsement or any affiliation with this book. Any trademarks (including, but not limiting to, screenshots) used in this book are solely used for editorial and educational purposes.

Table of Contents

Disclaimer: *Please note, while every effort has been made to ensure accuracy, this book is not endorsed by Alphabet, Inc. and should be considered unofficial.*

INTRODUCTION

Google's Pixel 8a is an exemplary piece of technology, offering a variety of features that cater to modern smartphone needs. This guide provides an introduction to this innovative device, walking you through its specifications, capabilities, and general functionalities to help you understand and enjoy the smartphone better.

DESIGN & BUILD

The Pixel 8a features a sturdy design with a glass front (protected by Gorilla Glass 3), an aluminum frame, and a plastic back. This combination provides durability and a comfortable grip. The dimensions of the device are 152 x 72.9 x 9 mm, and it weighs 193.5g, making it quite compact and lightweight.

This phone is IP67 dust and water-resistant, which means it can survive immersion in water up to 1 meter deep for 30 minutes. The device supports both Nano-SIM and eSIM for network connectivity.

DISPLAY

A 6.1-inch OLED screen graces the front of the Pixel 8a, with an impressive resolution of 1080 x 2400 pixels, leading to a clear, sharp, and vibrant display. The phone's 90Hz refresh rate ensures a smooth visual experience, whether you're scrolling through social media or playing games. The always-on display feature shows useful information like time and notifications, even when the phone is idle.

PERFORMANCE

The Pixel 8a runs on Android 13, powered by Google's own Tensor G2 chipset. It has an octa-core CPU setup for smooth multitasking and quick application launches. The GPU ensures graphical tasks like games and video playback run without a hitch.

This phone comes with an ample 128GB of internal storage and 8GB RAM, providing plenty of space for your apps, photos, and videos while also ensuring a swift and lag-free experience.

CAMERA

For photography enthusiasts, the Pixel 8a presents an impressive dual-camera setup. The 64 MP wide lens and 13 MP ultrawide lens work together to deliver sharp, detailed, and vibrant photos. The camera supports features like Dual-LED flash, Pixel Shift, Auto-HDR, and panorama, further enhancing your photography experience.

The device also excels in videography, offering 4K recording at 30/60fps. For selfie lovers, there's a 13 MP front camera that also supports Auto-HDR and panorama features.

CONNECTIVITY & SENSORS

The Pixel 8a supports Wi-Fi 802.11 a/b/g/n/ac/6e, Bluetooth 5.3, and has a built-in GPS system. Additionally, it offers Near Field Communication (NFC) technology, allowing for contactless transactions, pairing with other NFC devices, and more. There's a variety of sensors, including an under-display fingerprint sensor for secure unlocking, an accelerometer, a gyro sensor, a proximity sensor, a compass, and a barometer.

BATTERY

Powering the device is a non-removable Li-Po 4385 mAh battery, offering a substantial amount of usage time. The phone supports 18W wired charging and 7.5W wireless charging, ensuring your phone is back to full power in no time.

The Google Pixel 8a, available in Charcoal, Snow, Sea, and Coral, combines practical design with top-notch features, making it an excellent choice for anyone seeking to enjoy the latest in smartphone technology.

[1]

PIXEL 8A…WHAT'S THE BIG DIFFERENCE

Android 14 is the OS that comes packaged on the Pixel 8a, and it is a huge update. There are so many updates, that I'd have to write an entire book to cover them. Because many of them are small and not used by novice users, I won't do that. Instead, I'll go over the updates you are most likely to regularly use and appreciate. Throughout the book, I'll cover some of these in more detail. Below are the high-level updates to this newest OS:

- Lock Screen Reimagined: With Android 14, you can jazz up your lock screen. Swap out the clock, add weather updates, or even shuffle things around for a fresh look. Plus, you get to choose quick actions at the bottom.
- Sharing Made Easy: Sharing links, photos, or memes is now smoother. Apps can add their own special buttons to the share menu. So if you're in Chrome, you might see options to

send a link to your other devices or create a QR code.

- Step Up Your PIN: When you punch in your PIN, you'll see animations. It's not just about looks, though. If you use a six-digit PIN or longer, Android 14 lets your Pixel phone unlock the moment you key in the right PIN. No need for that extra "enter" button!

- Drag, Drop, and Swap Apps: Ever wished you could just drag text or an image from one app to another without the fuss? Android 14 makes it happen. Picture this: You're holding a fun meme in one app and seamlessly dropping it into your chat app. Smooth, right?

- Better Battery Life in Standby?: Android 14's all about giving your phone a longer rest. Some sneaky apps used to munch on your battery even when you weren't using them. Google's putting a stop to that. There's also smarter handling of notifications and alarms, meaning your phone won't have to wake up so often just to pass on a message.

- Screen Time: You used to have to go on a scavenger hunt to find out how much you used your phone. Android 14's making it a big deal by placing it right up top in battery stats. A great way to see how much you've been glued to your screen!

- Wallpapers Get Smarter: AI is everywhere...including wallpaper. You tell your phone what you fancy, maybe a sunset with flamingos, and voila!

WHY YOU SHOULD CARE ABOUT AI ON YOUR PIXEL 8A

AI seems to be everywhere these days, doesn't it? Phones are no exception. Google has been making big strides towards implementing AI into it's the devices, and the Pixel 8a is no exception.

AI is a big part of the Pixel 8a—one might even argue that it's the biggest update. Let's look at what AI is on the phone and why it's such a big deal. We'll dig in more to some of these topics later in the book.

Boosting Your Productivity

Google's new feature, Gemini, is a perfect example of AI designed to boost your creativity and productivity. This AI can understand the context of what you're doing on your phone—like drafting an email or searching for information. It can suggest content or even create images for you to include in emails or messages, all based on what you're currently working on. It's like having a co-pilot for your digital tasks.

Helping With Your Studies

For students, AI on the Pixel 8a can be a real lifesaver. Features like Circle to Search let you circle anything on your screen—say, a tough math problem—and get step-by-step help right then and there. No need to hop between apps or dig through textbooks; the information comes to you, making studying not just easier but more interactive.

Enhancing Accessibility

AI isn't just about convenience; it's also about accessibility. Later this year, updates to TalkBack powered by AI will provide richer descriptions of images for those who have low vision or are blind. Imagine getting spoken feedback that helps describe personal photos or online items accurately. This isn't just technology; it's technology that truly touches lives.

Keeping You Safe

Your Pixel 8a's AI also has a very serious role: keeping you safe. With new AI-driven features, your phone can alert you during a call if it detects patterns typical of scams. Say a fake bank representative tries to get your card details over the phone. Your Pixel 8a can give you a real-time heads-up to hang up and protect your information.

BATTLE OF THE PHONES

If you are like me you are probably overwhelmed by all the phones out there. iPhone, Samsung Galaxy…even Google have a whole fleet of devices. So what's the big difference?

This section will stack the Pixel 8a up against the most popular phones at a similar price point. It's not going to look at how it compares to phones like the iPhone 14 because it's not a fair comparison—they cost several times more, so, of course, they'll have more powerful features.

PIXEL VS PIXEL

Let's start with the Pixel 8. It's $200 more and probably the most obvious place you'll start when you're thinking about other phones—it's promoted on the same store page after all. So let's look at how they compare.

Both phones look sleek and are built to withstand the trials of everyday life. The Pixel 8a and Pixel 8 are nearly identical in size, but the Pixel 8 opts for a more premium feel with both a glass front and back, protected by the tougher Gorilla Glass Victus, compared to the Pixel 8a's Gorilla Glass 3 and plastic back. Additionally, the Pixel 8 is slightly more water-resistant, offering protection in up to 1.5 meters of water, which is a bit more than the 1 meter offered by the 8a.

Display and Visuals

On the surface, both phones have a similar OLED display with a high refresh rate of 120Hz, making everything from scrolling through websites to playing games look smoother. However, the Pixel 8's display is slightly bigger and offers HDR10+ with a higher brightness potential, which means it can show more details in dark and light areas and is easier to see in bright sunlight.

Performance and Storage

Underneath the surface, both phones run on the same Google Tensor G3 chip and offer the same memory options. This means in day-to-day tasks like opening apps, taking photos, and browsing the internet, both phones will perform similarly.

Cameras

This is where you'll see a notable difference. The Pixel 8 steps up with a 50 MP main camera compared to the 64 MP on the Pixel 8a. You might think higher numbers are better, but the Pixel 8's camera lets in more light and captures sharper details, thanks to larger pixels and advanced autofocus. It also offers a more sophisticated video and photo technology, making it a better choice for those who love photography.

Battery Life

The Pixel 8 comes with a slightly larger battery and more powerful charging options, meaning it not only lasts longer but also charges faster. It supports 27W wired and 18W wireless charging and even has reverse wireless charging, which can be handy for charging your other devices like earbuds on the go.

PIXEL 8A VS SAMSUNG

Samsung Galaxy is Samsung's bread and butter, but when your after a quality budget phone from Samsung, your probably thinking about the A55.

Let's take a look at how Pixel 8a compares to it.

The Pixel 8a and the Samsung A55 both offer modern designs and are built to last. The Pixel 8a has a mix of glass and aluminum with a plastic back, which keeps it lightweight yet durable. The Samsung A55, on the other hand, goes all in with glass on both the front and back and an aluminum frame, protected by the latest Gorilla Glass Victus+. It's slightly heavier but also gives off a more premium vibe. Both phones are water and dust resistant, which is great for peace of mind.

Screen Quality

Both phones boast high-quality displays, but they have some differences. The Pixel 8a has a 6.1-inch OLED screen, known for vibrant colors and deep blacks, with a high brightness and a smooth 120Hz refresh rate. The Samsung A55 features a slightly larger 6.6-inch Super AMOLED display, also with a 120Hz refresh rate and is capable of displaying HDR10+ content, which means movies and photos can look more dynamic and colorful.

Performance

The Pixel 8a runs on Google's own Tensor G3 chip, which is quite capable for handling everything from daily tasks to more intense gaming sessions. The Samsung A55 uses Samsung's Exynos 1480 processor, which also offers good performance but might lag behind in more demanding uses compared to the Tensor G3. Both are equipped with Android 14, but the Samsung layers on its own One UI, which might appeal if you like a more customized interface.

Camera Capabilities

Photography might be a deciding factor. The Pixel 8a features a dual-camera setup with a 64 MP main sensor, known for Google's color science and image processing capabilities. The Samsung A55 has a triple-camera system with a 50 MP main camera, adding a macro lens for close-up shots. This could give Samsung an edge if you enjoy taking diverse types of photos.

Battery Life & Charging

The Samsung A55 shines in battery life with a larger 5000 mAh battery compared to the 4492 mAh battery in the Pixel 8a. It also supports 25W wired charging, which is faster than the Pixel 8a's charging capabilities. This means you can spend less time tethered to an outlet with the A55.

Additional Features

Both phones lack a 3.5mm headphone jack but include stereo speakers and essential sensors. The Samsung A55 offers more versatility with its storage options and the inclusion of a microSD card slot, a nice perk if you like to keep lots of files and apps handy.

Price

Price is always a consideration. The Samsung A55 is generally less expensive than the Pixel 8a, making it potentially more appealing if you're looking for value and don't need the very latest chipset or Google's specific Android tweaks.

THE PIXEL 8A VS IPHONE 15

Finally, let's look at the iPhone 15. Apple does have a budget phone (the iPhone SE), but it hasn't been refreshed in over two years, so it's not the best comparison.

Design and Build

Both phones have sleek designs that feel modern and premium. The Pixel 8a has a glass front, an aluminum frame, and a plastic back, which might not feel as luxurious as the iPhone 15, which boasts a glass front and back with an aluminum frame. The iPhone also offers slightly better water resistance (up to 6 meters for 30 minutes compared to 1 meter for the Pixel), giving it an edge if you're particularly clumsy around water.

Display

Both devices feature a 6.1-inch screen, but the iPhone 15 uses Apple's Super Retina XDR OLED display which supports HDR10 and Dolby Vision, meaning colors and brightness can adjust better to give you the best viewing experience, especially when watching movies or playing games. The Pixel 8a's OLED screen is no slouch either, offering great color reproduction and a high peak brightness.

Performance and Storage

The iPhone runs on Apple's A16 Bionic chip, which is renowned for its efficiency and power, easily handling everything from high-end gaming to intensive multitasking. The Pixel 8a uses Google's Tensor G3 chip, which is also powerful but might lag slightly behind in some high-performance scenarios. Both phones offer similar storage options, but keep in mind, neither allows for expandable storage with an SD card.

Cameras

This is where both phones really try to stand out. The iPhone 15 features a dual-camera system with a 48 MP wide camera that captures stunning photos with great detail and color accuracy, and also supports advanced video features like Dolby Vision HDR recording. The Pixel 8a, while having a higher 64 MP wide camera, is known for Google's advanced image processing, making it fantastic for point-and-shoot photography, especially in challenging lighting conditions.

Battery and Charging

Battery life is crucial for many users. The iPhone 15 has a smaller battery than the Pixel 8a, but Apple's optimization means it generally lasts just as long. The iPhone also supports faster wired charging and dual wireless charging options (MagSafe and Qi2), which might be a plus if you already have an array of Apple-compatible accessories.

Ecosystem and Extras

Choosing between an iPhone and a Pixel often comes down to which ecosystem you prefer. The iPhone 15 integrates seamlessly with other Apple products, offering features like AirDrop, FaceTime, and continuity with Macs and iPads. The Pixel 8a shines with Google's integration, offering a seamless experience with services like Google Photos, Gmail, and Google Assistant.

UNDERSTANDING THE PIXEL 8A: IS IT THE RIGHT PHONE FOR YOU?

When considering a new smartphone, it's essential to match the phone's capabilities to your needs and expectations. The Google Pixel 8a is packed with features that aim to satisfy a broad range of users. But is it the right phone for you? Let's break down who the Pixel 8a is for, its limitations, and whether it's powerful enough for the average user.

Who is the Pixel 8a For?

The Everyday User: The Pixel 8a is built to handle all the essential tasks most users need. From browsing the internet and using apps to streaming video and music, its specs are more than adequate. The phone sports a robust Google Tensor G3 processor and 8GB of RAM, ensuring that everyday tasks are handled smoothly without lag.

Photography Enthusiasts: With a dual-camera setup featuring a 64 MP main camera and a 13 MP ultrawide camera, coupled with advanced features like dual-LED flash, Pixel Shift, and Auto-HDR, the Pixel 8a is a solid choice for photography enthusiasts who want a capable camera phone without breaking the bank.

Fans of Multimedia: The Pixel 8a's 6.1-inch OLED display with a 120Hz refresh rate and peak brightness of 2000 nits offers a vibrant viewing experience for watching videos and playing games. Additionally, stereo speakers enhance the audio experience, making it great for media consumption.

Who is the Pixel 8a Not For?

Power Users and Gamers: While the Pixel 8a is powerful, it might not satisfy users who need extreme performance for advanced gaming or intensive multitasking involving high-end applications. These users might find the GPU and the high-performance cores of the processor lacking when pushed to the limits.

Audiophiles and Wired Headphone Users: The absence of a 3.5mm headphone jack could be a dealbreaker for users who prefer using wired headphones without an adapter.

Expandable Storage Seekers: The Pixel 8a does not support microSD cards for storage expansion. Users who need more than the built-in 128GB or 256GB might find this limiting, especially if they handle large files directly on their device.

Is the Pixel 8a Powerful Enough for the Average User?

For the majority of smartphone users, the Pixel 8a offers more than enough power. Its modern chipset and ample RAM can handle daily activities such as social media, emails, regular apps, and casual gaming with ease. The device also supports 5G, ensuring that it is future-proof for the next several years with fast data speeds and improved connectivity.

Limitations

Despite its strengths, the Pixel 8a does have its limitations. It is not designed for extremely rugged environments (limited to IP67 rather than IP68), nor does it cater to those who prioritize having the absolute latest in phone camera technology or the most cutting-edge mobile gaming performance. Additionally, the battery life might be a concern for power users, as its 4492 mAh capacity may not last as long under heavy use compared to some other phones boasting larger batteries.

[2]

GETTING STARTED

SETUP

The setup is pretty intuitive, but there are still screens that might confuse you a little. If you are a self-starter and like just try things, then skip to the next section on the main UI elements of Android. If you want a more thorough walk-through, then read away!

Google knows you want to get started using your phone, so they've made the process pretty quick; most people will spend about 5 or 10 minutes.

The first thing you'll see is the "Hi there" screen; you could technically make an emergency call on this screen, but I don't recommend it unless it's really an emergency—this isn't a "hey, mom, I'll be late" emergency...this is a direct to emergency responders "I've fallen and can't get up" sort of call. When you are ready to get started, tap the blue "Start" button.

You have two options on the next screen: connect to wi-fi so you can start a "SIM-free" setup or insert your SIM card.

If you add a SIM card you can skip all of the next steps. If you are doing SIM-Free, then tap "Start SIM-free setup instead." The next screen explains SIM-free; SIM-free is exactly what it sounds like, but it's not supported by all carriers. If your carrier supports it, then I'd recommend doing it, as everything will be stored online vs. on a card that can be easily scratched and damaged. Tap the blue "Next" to begin.

SIM-free setup

If your mobile network uses SIM-free setup,
you'll get calls, texts, and data by downloading
an eSIM instead of inserting a SIM card.

The next screen prompts you to select your wi-fi network. This is followed by an update screen. It should take about a minute to get the latest update. When it's done, you'll see the "Copy apps & data" screen.

Copy apps & data
You can choose to transfer your apps, photos, contacts, Google Account, and more.

Copy apps and data is pretty resourceful. It will let you copy everything from your old phone so there's not as much to do on your new one—it works with both iPhone (through a special adaptor) and Android. It's not perfect—especially with the iPhone—but it will save you time. If you are coming from a previous generation Android phone, you can also do this without a cord by using your login. If you want to skip it and start from scratch, then select "Don't copy" in the lower left corner.

Find your old phone's cable

Use a cable that fits your old phone. This is usually the cable used for charging.

Insert cable into your old phone

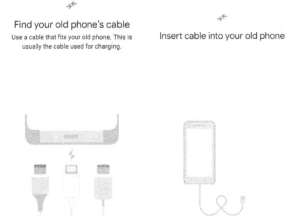

Next, sign in to your Google Account (the one you use the check email usually—unless you don't use Gmail). If you don't have a Google Account, then click the option to create it.

Google

Sign in

with your Google Account. Learn more

Email or phone

Forgot email?

Create account

Once you hit "next" and "sign in," you'll get a bunch of legal stuff. It's basically saying Google's not responsible for anything. Agree to it or you just bought yourself a very expensive brick. You'll see a lot of these legal screens, so either put on your reading glasses and settle in for a very long night, or just agree to them.

Google Services is the next screen. This is giving the phone permission to use features on the phone (like the fingerprint scanner, location services to see where you are at, send Google and developers crash reports, and back-up your phone to the Google Drive). I recommend selecting all of them. If you are worried about privacy, I'll show you some adjustments you can make later. I should also note: if you turn them off here, you can turn them back on later.

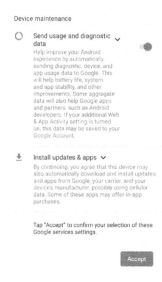

Next is yet another reminder that you can't blame Google for anything. They really want you to understand this. That way if the phone explodes in your hand, it's obviously your fault!

Additional legal terms

By clicking "I accept," you agree to the Google
Terms of Service and the Google Device
Arbitration Agreement.
Note: The Google Privacy Policy describes how
your data is handled.

All disputes regarding your Google device will
be resolved through **binding arbitration** on an
individual, non-class basis, as described in the
Google Device Arbitration Agreement, unless
you opt out by following the instructions in that
Agreement.

Next, it's time to start setting up your phone. What was all that other stuff? That was your account. First up to bat: your screen lock. This is basically so if someone steals or finds your phone, they can't open it unless they know your password.

Set screen lock

For security, set PIN

PIN must be at least 4 digits

Screen lock options

If you tap on "Screen lock options" you will see even more options. The unlock can be a pattern (e.g. move in the shape of a seven), it can be a word, or it could be a number (but don't use your bank pin number!). You can also skip adding a pin and have your phone always un-locked.

The next screen will ask you for a pin. If you tap "Screen lock options" you can also add a pattern. It's all a preference. My only advice is not to use a pin you use somewhere else (like a bank pin) or an easy pin (like 1234).

Once you hit "Next," and then reenter the pin to confirm it.

You'll also have the option for adding a fingerprint to unlock your phone. Unlike a lot of phones, the Pixels fingerprint sensor is on the screen itself. Pretty cool right? Here's a nugget of advice, however. If you are like me, you'll probably put a screen protector over it so there's more protection if it falls. That's going to be problematic for your sensor until you update it—so if you are finding it's not working, then update the Android software (I'll show you how later) and see if that fixes it.

Adding a finger print is pretty simple. The phone will tell you exactly where your finger should go. Just tap your finger to the screen where shown. That's it! You can add one finger or several. You can also add other people's fingers—so if you have someone who you give permission to use your phone, then you can add them as well.

Just tap Add Another at the end of the setup if you want to add more.

New to Pixel 7 is the ability to unlock with your face; this is something that's been missing sense the Pixel 4.

Configuring Google Assistant is next. Google Assistant is the Google equivalent of Siri. You can tap "Leave & get reminder" but it's very quick to do, so it's best to just get it out of the way.

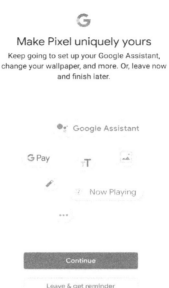

Once you agree to the terms, you are ready to go. You'll be asked a few questions (unless you have a Google Home and Google already knows your voice).

You are just about done! The "Anything else?" screen is your last chance to add in settings before finishing the set up—and remember: you can change all this later. So if you don't want to do it now, you always can do it later. The one thing I will point out is "Add another email account"; if you are using this phone at work, then it's a good idea to add in your work email here.

The last screen is asking if you'd like to get tip emails from Google about how to use your phone. When you are first getting started, these emails are helpful. They don't come very often. If you want to turn it on, then just toggle the "sign up" button to on (it will turn blue—or be blue if it's already checked).

After a few seconds, a screen will appear that says, "Go Home." Kind of sounds like the phone is telling you that you didn't pass the setup and now must go home empty handed.

Don't worry! It's just telling you to go to the Home screen because you are finally done. These final screens are short tutorials that will give you a couple tips for how the phone works.

After a few tips, you'll see the "All set!" screen, which is the final screen. You are finally done!

Swipe up and you will see your Home screen. You are finally ready to use your phone!

FINDING YOUR WAY AROUND

People come to the Pixel from all sorts of different places: iPhone, other Android phone, flip phone, two styrofoam cups tied together with string. This next section is a crash course in the interface. If you've used Android before, then it might seem a little simple, so skip ahead if you already know all of this.

If any of this seems a little rushed, there's good reason: it is! We'll cover these points in more detail later. This is just a quick starter / reference.

On the bottom of your screen is the shortcut bar—you'll be spending a lot of time here; you can add whatever you want to this area, but these are the apps Google thinks you'll use most—and, with the exception of the Play Store, they are probably right. Depending on the settings you've picked and the phone you have, it may or may not look different. It could show four apps in a row instead of six, for example.

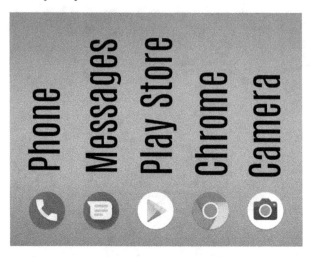

So, what are these? Real quick, these are as follows:

- **Phone**: Do you want to take a wild guess what the phone button does? If you said brings you an ice cream, then maybe you aren't cut out for a phone. But if you said something along the lines of "It launches an app to call people" then you'll have no problem at all with your new device. Surprise, surprise: this pricey gadget that plays games, takes pictures, and keeps you up to date on political ramblings on social media does one more interesting thing: it calls people!

- **Message**: Message might be a little more open-ended than "Phone"; that could mean email message, text messages, messages you keep getting on your bathroom mirror to put the toilet seat down. In this case, it means "text messages" (but really—put that toilet seat down...you aren't doing anyone any favors). This is the app you'll use whenever you want to text cute pictures of cats.

- **Play Store**: Anything with the word "Play" in the title must be fun, right?! This app is what you'll use to download all those fun apps you always hear about.
- **Chrome**: Whenever you want to surf the Internet, you'll use Chrome. There are actually several apps that do the same thing—like Firefox and Opera—but I recommend Chrome until you are comfortable with your phone. Personally, I think it's the best app for searching the Internet, but you'll soon learn that most things on the phone are about preference, and you may find another Internet browser that suits your needs more.
- **Camera**: This apps opens pictures of vintage cameras...just kidding! It's how you take pictures on your phone. You use this same app for videos as well.

Next to the shortcut bar, the area you'll use the most is the notification bar. This is where you'll get, you guessed it, notifications! What's a notification? That's any kind of notice you have elected to receive. A few examples: text message alerts, email alerts, amber alerts, and apps that have updates.

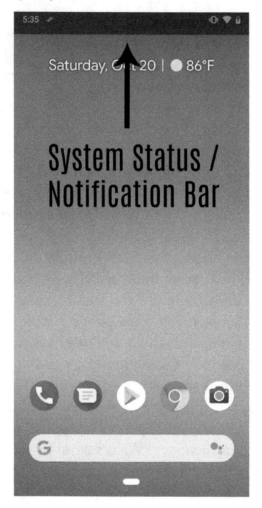

When you drag your finger down from the notification bar, you'll get a list of several settings that you can adjust. Press and hold any of these options and you'll open an app with even more options.

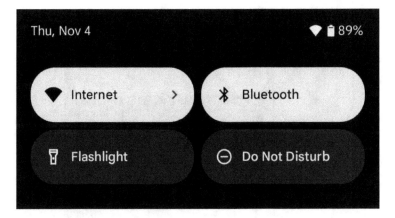

From right to left these are the options you can change or use:

- Wi-fi
- Bluetooth
- Do not disturb
- Flashlight

If you continue dragging down, this thin menu expands and there are a few more options.

The first is at the top of the screen—it's the slider, and it makes your device brighter or dimmer depending on which way you drag it.

You can slide your finger to see more options:

- Auto-Rotate – Locks (unlocks) the device from rotating
- Battery Saver – Puts the device in a low energy mode for extended battery life, but not as great processing power.
- Screen cast – Beams the screen to another device—like a Google TV.
- Screen Record – Screen recording used to be something you needed a special app for; Android 11 brought native recording. So you can record what you are doing on your screen and share it with someone else. It's great for tutorial videos. You are also able to use your phone's microphone to narrate with your voice.
- Nearby share

- Camera / Mic Disable – Quickly turn off your camera or mic.

Near the bottom on the left, is a little pencil edit button. That let's you reorganize what options are shown where.

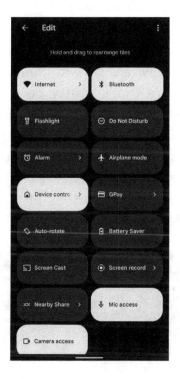

Scroll a little more and you'll see even more quick settings that you can add to the notification bar. Among them:

- **Data** – Tapping this turns your data on and off, which is handy if you are running low on data and don't want to be charged extra for it.

- **Night light** - This is a special mode that dims your screen and makes the screen appropriate for reading in dark settings.
- **Battery share** – when you press this, you can use your device like a wireless charger. What does that mean? Let's say your friend has an iPhone with wireless charging and they're almost out of battery. You can press this, then hold their phone against yours and share your battery wirelessly with them.

Something else that's pretty cool on this notification area: you can see a history of notifications.

If you get a lot of notifications, you probably have accidentally dismissed something that you didn't mean to. Now you can see what it was.

To use it, go to the bottom of all your notifications, then select "Manage."

From here, toggle "Use notification history" to on.

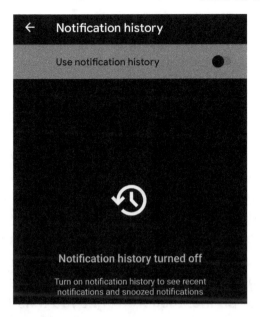

Now when you go back to that same area "Manage" is replaced with "History."

FEELING HOME-LESS?

You may have noticed something that seems important missing from your phone: a Home button. On older phones, this was a critical button that gets you to the Home screen whenever you push it.

How on Earth do you get Home without a Home button?! Easy. Are you ready? Swipe up. That's it!

If you've used any Apple device, then you might know a thing or two about Siri. She's the assistant that "sometimes" works; Google has its own version of Siri and it's called Google Assistant. The names not quite as creative as Siri, but many say it works better. I'll let you be the judge of that.

To get to the Google Assistant from anywhere, just say "Ok, Google." If you are on the Home screen, then there's also a Google Assistant widget. This little bar does more than make appointments and get your information—it's also a global search. What does that mean? It means you can type in anything you want to know, and it will search both the Internet and your phone. If it's a contact in your phone, then it will get you that. But if it's the opening hours for the Museum of Strange then it will search the Internet—it will also give you a map of the location and the phone number.

GET AROUND ON YOUR PIXEL PHONE

When it comes to getting around your Pixel, learning how to use gestures will be the quickest, most effective method. You can change some of the gesture options by going to the Settings app, then System > Gestures > System navigation.

The most important gesture is how to get back to the Home screen—there are no buttons after all. That's the easiest one to remember: swipe up from the bottom of the screen.

When you are on an Internet page, you can swipe from the left or right edge of the screen to go backwards or forwards.

To select text, tap and hold over the text, then lift your finger when it responds.

MULTITASKING

Those are the easy gestures to remember; if you want to move around quickly, however, you need to know the two big multitask gestures, which help you switch between apps.

The first is to see your open apps. To do this, swipe up like you're going to the Home screen, but keep going until about the middle of the screen and then stop and lift your finger—don't make a quick swipe-up gesture like you would when going Home. This will show you previews of all of your open apps, and you can swipe between them. Tap the one you want to open.

The quickest way to switch back and forth between two or three apps, however, is to swipe from left to right along the bottom edge of the screen. This swipes between apps in the order that you have used them.

ZOOM

Need to see text bigger? There are two ways to do that. Note: this works on many, but not all apps.

The first way is to pinch to zoom.

r with the Additic
between you an
es. It is importan
Collectively, this l
s".

etween what the
al Terms say, ther
elation to that Se

The second way is to double tap on the text.

ROTATE

You probably have noticed if you rotate your phone, it rotates the screen. What if you don't want to rotate the entire screen? You can turn that off very easily. Swipe down and then tap the "arrows" button to enable or disable it.

[3]

THE RIDICULOUSLY SIMPLE OVERVIEW OF ALL THE THINGS YOU SHOULD KNOW

This chapter will cover:
- Customizing screens
- Split screens
- Gestures

MAKING PRETTY SCREENS

If you've used an iPhone or iPad, then you may notice the screen looks a little...bare. There's literally nothing on it. Maybe you like that. If so, then good for you! Skip ahead. If you want to decorate that screen with shortcuts and widgets, then read on. Since Android 12 made things more about you than ever before, prepare to have more control than ever before!

ADDING SHORTCUTS

Any app you want on this screen, just find it, and then press and hold; when a menu comes up, drag it upward until the screen appears and move it to where you want it to go. You can also drag it to new screens.

To remove an app from a screen, tap and hold, then drag it upward to the "Remove" text that appears when you move it up. When it's there, let go.

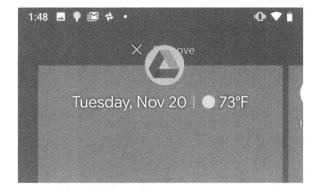

WIDGETS

Shortcuts are nice, but widgets are better. Widgets are sort of like mini-programs that run on your screen. A common widget people put on their screen is the weather forecast. Throughout the day the widget will update automatically with up-to-date info.

To add a widget, go to the screen you want to add it to and tap and hold until the menu comes up.

Select "Widgets." This opens up a widget library—it's like a mini app store.

When you find one you want to add, tap and hold it, then drag it to the screen you want to add it to.

Widgets come in all sorts of shapes and sizes, but most of them can be resized. To resize it, tap and hold it. If you see little circles, then you can tap those and drag it in or out to make it bigger or smaller.

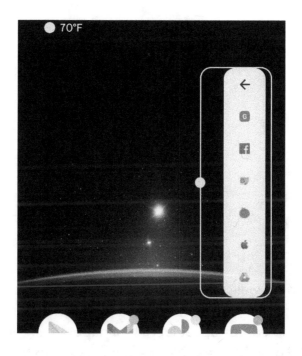

You remove widgets the same way you remove short-cuts. Tap and hold and then drag it upward to the re-move.

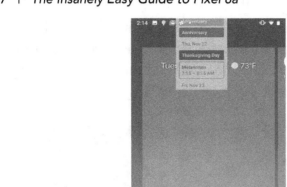

WALLPAPER

Adding wallpaper to your screen is done in a similar way. Tap and hold your finger on the Home screen, when the menu comes up, select "Wallpaper" instead of "Widgets." Some of the options even move—so the wallpaper always has something moving across your screen—it's like a slow moving movie.

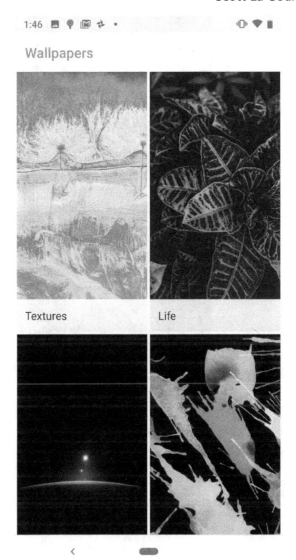

When you have a wallpaper open that you want to add, just hit the "Set Wallpaper" in the upper right corner.

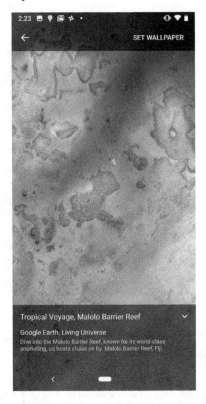

You can also change the style of your phone—such as the colors.

A WORD, OR TWO, ABOUT MENUS

It's pretty intuitive that if you tap on an icon, it opens the app. What's not so obvious is if you tap and hold there are other options. Every app is different. Usually, they're shortcuts—tapping and holding over the Phone icon, for example, brings up your favorites; doing the same thing over the camera brings up a selfie mode shortcut. Tap and hold over your favorite apps to see what shortcuts are available.

SPIT SCREENS

The Pixel phone comes in two different sizes; the bigger screen obviously gives you a lot more space, which makes split screen apps a pretty handy feature. It works on the smaller Pixel as well, though it doesn't feel as effective on the smaller screen.

To use this feature, swipe up to bring up multitasking; next, tap the icon above the window you want to turn into split screen (note: this feature is not supported on all apps); if split screen is available, you'll see a menu that has an option for split screen.

Once you tap "split screen," it will let you swipe left and right to find the app you want to split the screen with. Tap the one you want.

Your screen is now split in two.

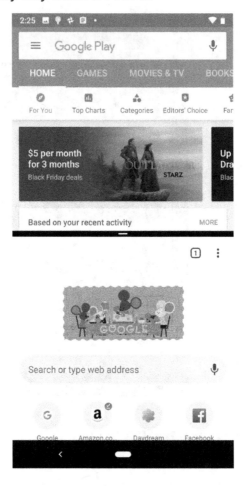

That thin black bar in the middle is adjustable; you can move it up or down so one of the apps has more screen real estate.

To exit this mode, drag the black bar either all the way to the top or all the way to the bottom until one of the apps completely goes away.

GESTURES

JUMP TO CAMERA

Press the power button twice to quickly jump to the camera.

FLIP CAMERA

Switch in and out of selfie mode while you are in the camera by double-twisting the phone.

DOUBLE-TAP

If your phone is in standby, double-tap the screen and the time and notifications will appear.

GOOGLE ASSISTANT

Google Assistant can be trigged by saying "Hey, Google". With gestures, there's a new way: swipe from either the right or left bottom corner.

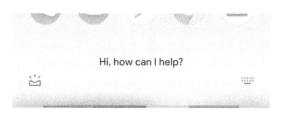

Hi, how can I help?

[4]

THE BASICS...AND KEEP IT RIDICULOUSLY SIMPLE

This chapter will cover:
- Making calls
- Sending messages
- Finding and downloading apps
- Driving directions

Now that you have your phone set up and know your way around the device at its most basic level, let's go over the apps you'll be using the most that are currently on your shortcut or favorite bar:
- Phone

- Messages
- Google Play Store
- Chrome

Notice that Camera is off this list? There's a lot to cover with Camera, so I'll go over it in a separate chapter.

Before we get into it, there's something you need to know: how to open apps not on your favorite bar. It's easy. From your home screen, swipe up from the bottom. Notice that menu that's appearing? That's where all the additional apps are.

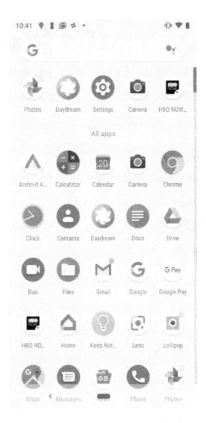

MAKING CALLS

So...who you going to call? Ghostbusters?!

You would be the most awesome person in the world if Ghostbusters was in your phone contacts! But before you can find that number in your contacts, it would probably help to know how to add a contact, find a contact, edit a contact, and put contacts into groups, right? So before we get to making calls, let's do baby steps and cover Contacts.

CONTACTS

So, let's open up the Contacts app to get started. See it? Not on your favorite bar, right? So where is it?! That's why I showed you earlier how to get to additional apps. Swipe up from the bottom of your screen and keep swiping until the menu appears in its entirety.

It's in alphabetical order, so the Contacts app is in the C's. It looks like this:

Contacts

Chances are if you've added your email account, you'll already have a lot of contacts listed. Like hundreds!

You can either scroll slowly, or head to the right-hand side of the app and scroll—this lets you quickly scroll by letters. Just slide your finger until you see the letter of the contact you want and then stop.

I'm getting ahead of myself, however! Before you can scroll, it would be nice to know how to add a contact so there are people to scroll to. To add a contact, tap on that blue plus sign.

Adding a person looks more like applying for a job than adding a contact. There are rows and rows of fields!

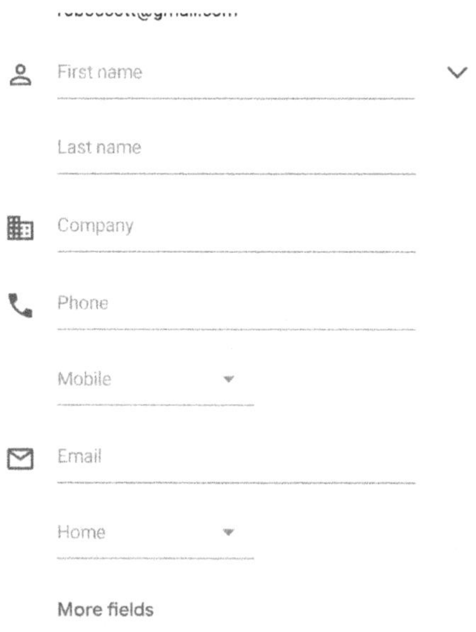

First name ⌄

Last name

Company

Phone

Mobile ▾

Email

Home ▾

More fields

Just in case you weren't overwhelmed by all the fields, you can tap more fields and get even more!

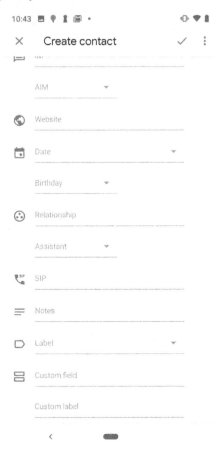

Is that not enough? Google has you covered because you can add a custom field!

Here's the most important thing you need to know: fields are optional! You can add a name and email and that's it. You don't even have to add their phone number. If you want to call them, then that would certainly help though.

If you have a hard time remembering who people are, then you can also take a picture or add a picture you already have. Comes in handy if you have eight kids and you can't remember if Joey is the one with blonde hair or red hair.

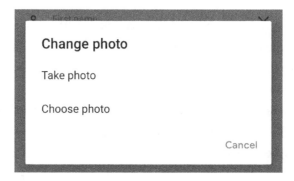

Once you are done, tap the checkbox. That saves it. If you decide you don't want to add a contact after all, the tap the X. That closes it without saving.

EDITING A CONTACT

If you add an email and then later decide you should add a phone number, or if you want to edit anything else, then just find the name in your contacts and tap it once. This brings up all the info you've already added.

Go to the lower corner and tap on the pencil button. This makes the contact editable. Go to your desired field and update. When you are finished, tap the checkbox in the upper right corner.

SHARING A CONTACT

If you have your phone long enough, someone will ask you for so and so's phone number. The old-fashioned way was to write it down. But you have a smartphone, so you aren't old-fashioned!

The new way to share a number is to find the person in your contacts, tap their name, then tap those three dots in the upper right corner of your screen. This brings up a menu.

Delete

Share

Add to Home screen

Set ringtone

Route to voicemail

Help & feedback

There are a few options here, but the one you want is "Share"; from here you have a few options, but the easiest is to text or email the contact to your friend. This sends them a contact card. So if you have other information with that contact (such as email) then that will be sent over as well.

DELETE CONTACT

There are a few more options on that menu I just showed. If you decide a person is dead to you and you never want to contact them again, then you can return to that menu and tap "Delete." This erases them from your phone, but not your life.

GET ORGANIZED

Once you start getting lots of contacts, then it's going to make finding someone more time-consuming. Labels helps. You can add a label for "Family" for instance, and then stick all of your family members there.

When you open your contacts and tap those three lines in the upper left corner, you'll see a menu. This is where you'll see your labels. So with labels, you can jump right into that list and find the contact you need.

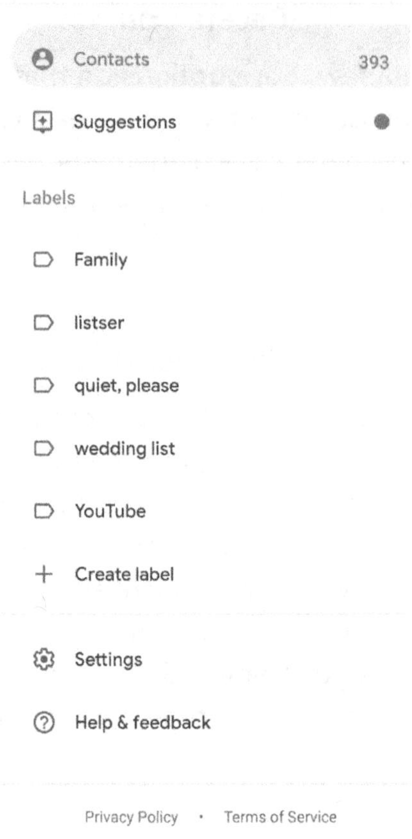

😔 Contacts		393
⊕ Suggestions		●

Labels

▱ Family

▱ listser

▱ quiet, please

▱ wedding list

▱ YouTube

+ Create label

⚙ Settings

⊘ Help & feedback

Privacy Policy · Terms of Service

You can also send the entire group inside the label an email or text message. So for instance, if your child is turning 2 and you want to remind everyone in your "Family" contact not to come, then just tap on that label, and then tap on the three dots in the upper right corner. This brings up a menu of options.

Send email

Send message

Remove contacts

Rename label

Delete label

From here, just tap send email or send message.

But what if you don't have labels? Or if you want to add people to a label? Easy. Remember that long application you used to add a contact? One of the fields was called "Labels." You have to tap more to see it. It's all the way at the bottom. One of the last fields, in fact.

If you've never added a label or want to add a new one, then just start typing. If you have another one that you'd like to use, then just tap the arrow and select it.

When you are done, don't forget to tap "Save."

DELETE LABEL

If you decide you no longer want to have a label, then just go to the menu I showed you above—side menu, then the three dots. From here, tap the "Delete Label."

If there's just one person you want to boot from the label, then tap them and go to the label and delete it.

MAKING CALLS

That concludes our sidetrack into the Contacts app. We can now return to getting back to making phone calls to the Ghostbusters.

You can make a call by opening the Contacts app, then selecting the contact, and then tapping on their phone number. Alternatively, you can tap on the Phone button from your Home screen or favorite bar.

There are a few options when you open this app. Let's talk about each one.

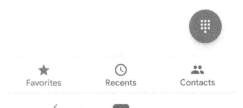

Starting from the far left is the Favorites tab. If you tap this, then you'll see your favorite contacts. If you haven't added any, then this will be empty. If you want to make someone your favorite, then tap them in your Contacts, and tap the star on the top by their name. Once you do that, they'll automatically start showing up here.

In the middle is the Recents tab. If you've made any calls, they'll show here.

The last option is Contacts, which opens a version of the Contacts app that's within the Phone app.

Also on the right is the dial button.

If you want to dial someone the old-fashioned way by tapping in numbers, then tap this.

1 ꝋ	2 ABC	3 DEF
4 GHI	5 JKL	6 MNO
7 PQRS	8 TUV	9 WXYZ
*	0 +	#

When you are done with the call, hit the "End" button on your phone.

Answer and Decline Calls

What do you do when someone calls you? Probably ignore it because it's a telemarketer!

It's easy to accept a call, however. When the phone rings, the number will appear and if the person is in your Contacts, then the name will appear as well. To answer, just swipe the "answer." To decline just drag the "decline."

Play Angry Birds While Talking to Angry Mom

What if you're on a call with your mom and she's just complaining about something, but you don't want to be rude and hang up? Easy. You multitask! This means you could play Angry Birds while talking!

To multitask, just swipe up from the bottom of your phone, and open the app you want to work in while you are talking. The call will show in the notification area. Tap it to return to the call.

DIRECT MY CALL

Direct My Call came out in 2021 as a way to help you quickly navigate automated menus. The AI on the Pixel 7 is able to detect the menus and put a call menu on your screen, which makes it easier to get where you want to go before the voice on the line says it. It's a feature that will improve over time, so it may not work as expected at first.

To use it, open the Phone app, then tap the three-dot menu icon in the upper corner and select "Settings." Go to "Direct My Call" then toggle it on.

HOLD FOR ME

Google Assistant has become quite literally, your assistant. This is especially true on phone calls. Have you ever been on hold for way too long? Google Assistant knows your pain and is willing to hold for you! It will tell you when it detects a human has picked up. To use it, open the Phone app, tap the three-dot menu in the upper-right corner and select "Settings." Last, tap "Hold for Me."

DON'T BE SPAMMY

Nobody likes that call asking if you want to buy something. Google can help filter your calls and get rid of spam. To turn it on go to the Phone app, then tap those three dots in the upper right corner, and tap settings. Go to "Spam and Call Screen." Tap the toggle next to "See caller and spam ID".

MESSAGES

Now that you know how Contacts and Phone works, messaging will be like second nature. They share many of the same properties.

Let's open up the Messages app (it's on your Favorites bar).

CREATE / SEND A MESSAGE

When you have selected the contact(s) to send a message to, tap Compose. You can also manually type in the number in the text field.

You can add more than one contact--this is known as a group text.

Use the text field to type out your message. If you want to add anything fancy to your message (like photos or gifs) then tap the plus sign. This brings up a menu with more options.

When you are ready to send your message, tap the arrow with the SMS under it.

VIEW MESSAGE

When you get a message, your phone will vibrate, chirp, or do nothing—it all depends on how you set up your phone. To view the message, you can either open the app, or swipe down to see your notifications—one will be the text message.

CONVERSATIONS

Google took big strides in Android 11 to make replying to messages more streamlined and effortless.

One place you see this is with Conversations. When you get a message (text, Facebook message, Twitter message, etc), you'll see that in your notification area by swiping down from the top.

The old method was to click that message to reply. Now you can see the message, set the priority level, and reply right from this area.

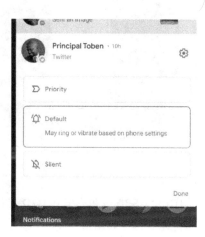

CHAT BUBBLES

Another area you'll see Android 11 streamline approach to messages is with Chat Bubbles. Chat Bubbles will appear on the side of whatever app you are working in, so you can reply without actually closing the app. As the name suggests, they'll be little bubbles on the side of your screen.

If you aren't crazy about this feature, you can toggle it off by going to the Settings app, then Apps & Notifications> Notifications > Bubbles.

SMART REPLY

If you're a Gmail user, you've probably started to see Smart Replies in your email. Smart Reply uses a computer engine to recognize what you will type next and make a suggestion.

Smart Reply works so surprisingly well you might be a little creeped out by it—like it will feel like some person is on the other end of the screen reading your messages! That's not the case. It's all artificial Intelligence. But if you still find the feature either creepy or annoying then you can go to the Settings app, then search for Smart Reply. Under Suggestions in chat, you'll see a on / off toggle for the feature.

WHERE'S AN APP FOR THAT?

I mentioned earlier that you could play Angry Birds while talking to your angry mom on the phone. Sound fun? But where is Angry Birds on your phone? It's not! You have to download it.

Adding and removing apps on the Pixel is easy. Head to your favorite bar on the bottom of your Home screen and tap the Google Play app.

This launches the Play Store.

From here you can browse the top apps, see editors' picks, look through categories, or, if you have an app in mind, search for it. The Play Store isn't just for apps. You can use the tabs on the top to go to movies, books, and music. Any kind of downloadable content that's offered by Google can be found here.

When you see the app you want, tap on it. You can read through reviews, see screenshots, and install it on your phone. To install, simply tap the install button—if it's a paid app you'll be prompted to buy it. If there's no price, it's free (or offers in-app payments—which means the app is free, but there are premium features inside it you may have to pay for).

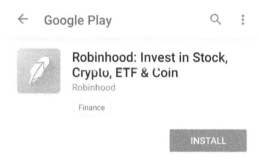

The app is now stored in the app section of your device (remember the section you get to when you swipe up from the bottom to the top?).

REMOVE APP

If you decide you no longer want an app, go to the app in the app menu and tap and hold it. This brings up a box that says "App info." Tap that.

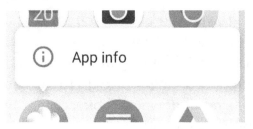

From this menu, you'll get all the information about the app; one of the options is to remove it. Tap that and you're done.

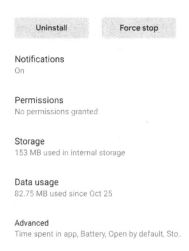

If you download the app from the Play Store, you can always delete it. Some apps that were pre-installed on your phone cannot be deleted.

DRIVING DIRECTIONS

Back in the day, you may have had a GPS. It was a fancy plastic device that would give you directions for anywhere in North America. You can throw out that device because your phone is your new GPS.

To get directions, swipe up to open up your apps. Tap the Maps app.

Maps

It's automatically going to be set to wherever you are currently at—which is both creepy and useful.

To get started, just type where you want to go. I'm searching for an amusement park in Anaheim.

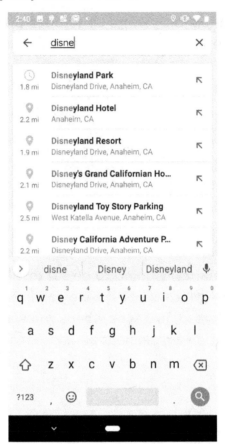

It automatically starts filling in what it thinks you are going to type and tells you the distance. When you see the one you want, tap it.

It pinpoints the location on the map and also gives you an option to call, share or get directions to the location. If you want to zoom out or in, just use two fingers and pinch in or out on the screen.

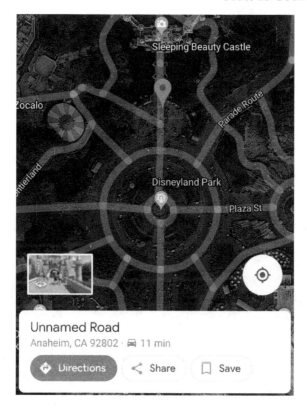

It automatically gets directions from where you are. Want it from a different location? Just tap on the "Your location" field and type where you want to go. You can also reverse the directions by tapping on the double arrows. When you are ready to go, tap "Start."

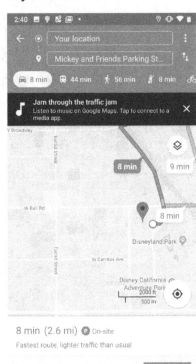

What if you don't want to drive? What if you want to walk? Or bike? Or take a taxi? There are options for all of those and more! Tap the slider under the address bar to whatever you prefer. This updates the directions—when you walk, for example, it will show you one-way streets and also update the time it will take you.

What if you want to drive but are like me: terrified of freeways in California? There's an option to avoid highways. Tap the menu button in the upper right corner of the screen, then select what you want to avoid, and hit "done." You are now rerouted to a longer route—notice how the times probably changed?

Once you get your directions, you can swipe up to get turn-by-turn directions. You can even see what it looks like from the street. It's called Street View.

Street View isn't only for streets. Google is expanding the feature everywhere. If you hold your finger over the map, there will be an option to show Street View if it's available. Just tap the thumbnail. Here's a Street View:

You can wander around the entire park! If only you could ride the rides, too! You can get even closer to the action by picking up the Dreamview headset. When you stick your phone in that, you can turn your head and the view turns with you.

Street View is also available in a lot of malls and other tourist attractions. Point your map to the Smithsonian in Washington, DC and get a pretty cool Street View.

WHAT'S THE NAME OF THAT SONG?

We've all had that moment where we are sitting in a coffee shop or standing in an elevator and that "one" song plays. The one we love or hate or just want to know the name to. Yes, there's an app to tell us the name, but sometimes we can't pull it out in time—or we just don't want yet another app on our phone. That's where Now Playing comes in handy.

Now Playing has been around since the Pixel 2, but it often goes unnoticed. It detects music playing around you and adds them to a list that you can look at later. It's all in the background and you don't even know it's running unless you've set up notifications.

To see the songs that have been recorded in your log, go to Settings > Sound > Now Playing. You can see your log by clicking on the history, or you can toggle on the "show songs on lock screen" button.

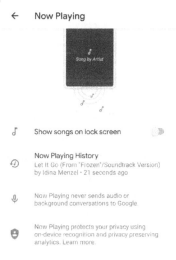

LIVE CAPTIONING

One of the bigger features to Android 10 is live captioning; live captioning can transcribe any video you record and show what's being said. It works surprisingly well and is pretty accurate.

To turn it on, go to Settings > Sound > Live Caption.

In the settings, you can also toggle off profanity, and, coming soon, select a different language. If it's something you'd only occasionally use, I recommend leaving it toggled off, but having it toggle on under Live Caption in volume control. With that toggled on, all you have to do is press the volume button. Once you do that, you'll see the option to turn it on; it's the bottom option.

Once it's on, you'll start seeing a transcription appear in seconds.

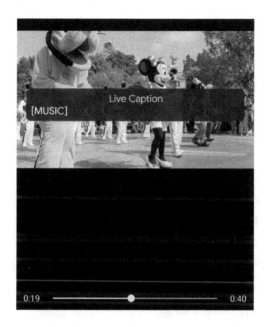

REFRESH RATE

The Pixel 5 supports up to 90Hz refresh rate. Wow, right? Actually, most people have no idea what this means. It's frames per second (FPS)—or 90 FPS. So, what does that mean? If you're playing games or using something that has fast moving action, it means things will seem a lot smoother. It will also eat your battery life to shreds, so use with caution (60Hz is the norm).

To toggle it on / off there are two options. The first way is to go to Settings > Display > Advanced > Smooth Display. This is going to turn it on / off automatically.

If you want to force it on, then there's a second option. Note: this option is "use at your own risk" because it's a developer option. My advice is not to use it unless you know what you are doing. To do it, go to Settings > About phone; go to the very bottom and tap the Build number several times until you are in developer mode. Now go to System > Advanced > Developer Options > Force 90Hz refresh rate.

SHARING WI-FI

Anytime you have guests over, you almost always get the question: what's your wi-fi password. If you are like me, then it probably annoys you. Maybe your password is really long, maybe you just don't like giving out your password, or maybe you are just too embarrassed to say that it's "Feet$FetishLover1." Whatever the reason, then you will love sharing your wi-fi with QR codes. Gone are the days of giving this info out. Just give them a code that they scan, and they'll have access without ever knowing what your password is.

To use it, go to your wi-fi settings, then select the configure button for the wi-fi you want to share.

This will bring up your wi-fl info; tap the blue "Share" option with the QR code.

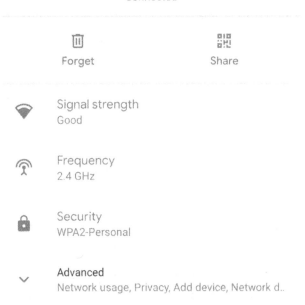

Once you verify that it's you, then you will see the code to scan and you just have to show it to your friend.

SCREENSHOT

If you've ever run into a problem with your phone and they said, "Take a Screenshot of it" then what they mean on Android is to hold your power button and volume down at the same time. That will screenshot whatever is on your screen and put it in a folder in your photos. Just click library when you open your photo album and you'll see a folder called screenshots.

When you do power + volume down, you'll see a preview appear in your lower left corner. It will disappear in a few seconds, unless you tap that you want to edit it.

If the screen allows it (not all will, so don't get frustrated if you don't see this option at first), you can capture more than what's on your screen; it's called a scrolling screenshot. If available, then you'll see a button that says Capture More. This kind of capture is great for long, text heavy, webpages.

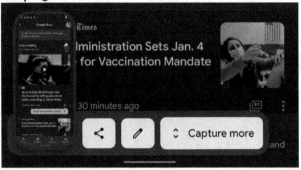

When you tap Capture more, you'll be given the option to drag over the area you want to capture more of. You can do the entire page or just part of it.

GOOGLE RECORDER

Google Recorder has always been a student dream by transcribing what is being recorded automatically. It gets better with the Pixel 7 (though the feature was not available at this writing) by letting you label who's speaking; if, for example, you have an interview with several people, it will detect who is saying what.

[5]

LET'S GO SURFING NOW!

This chapter will cover:
- Setting up email
- Creating and sending email
- Managing multiple accounts
- Browsing the Internet

When it comes to the Internet, there are two things you'll want to do:
- Send email
- Browse the Internet

ADD AN EMAIL ACCOUNT

When you set up your phone, you'll set it up to your Google Account, which is usually your email.

You may, however, want to add another email account—or remove the one you set up.

To add an email, swipe up to bring up your apps, and tap on "Settings."

Next, tap on "Accounts."

From here, select "Add Account"; you can also tap on the account that's been set up and tap remove account—but remember you can have more than one account on your phone.

Once you add your email, you'll be asked what type of email it is. Follow the steps after you select the email type to add in your email, password, and other required fields.

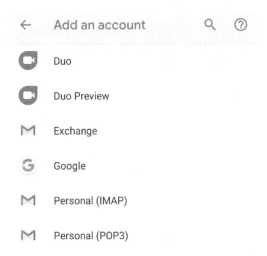

CREATE AND SEND AN EMAIL

To send an email using Gmail (Pixel's native email app), swipe up to get to your apps, tap "Gmail," and tap "Compose a New Email" (the little round red pencil in the lower right corner). When you're done, tap the send button.

You can also use the Google Play Store to find other email apps (such as Outlook).

MANAGE MULTIPLE EMAIL ACCOUNTS

If you have more than one Gmail account, tap the three lines at the upper left of your email screen; this brings out a slider menu. If you tap on the little arrow next to the email address, it drops down and will show other accounts. If none are listed, you can add one.

SURFING THE INTERNET

Google's native Web browser is Chrome. You can use other browsers (which can be found in the Google Play Store). This book will only cover Chrome, however.

Get started by tapping on the Chrome browser icon from your favorite bar, or by going into all programs.

If you've used Chrome on a desktop or any other device, then this chapter won't exactly be rocket science—just like the email app, many of the same properties you find on the desktop exist on the mobile version.

When you open it, you'll see it's a pretty basic browser. There are three main things that you'll want to note.

- **Address Bar** - As you would guess, this is where you put the Internet address you want to go to (google.com, for example); what you should understand, however is that this is not just an address bar. This is a search bar. You can use it to search for things just as you would searching for something on Google; when you hit the enter key, it takes you to the Google search results page.

- **Tab Button** - Because you are limited in space, you don't actually see all your tabs like you would on a normal browser; instead you get a button that tells you how many tabs are open. If you tap it, you can either toggle between the tabs, or swipe over one of the pages to close the tab.

- **Menu Button** - The last button brings up a menu with a series of other options that I'll talk about next.

→ ☆ ↓ ⓘ ↻

New tab

New incognito tab

Bookmarks

Recent tabs

History

Downloads

Share...

Find in page

Add to Home screen

Desktop site   ☐

Settings

Help & feedback

The menu is pretty straightforward, but there are a few things worth noting.

"New incognito tab" opens your phone into private browsing; that doesn't mean your IP isn't tracked. It means your history isn't record; it also means passwords and cookies aren't stored.

A little bit further down is "History"; if you want your history erased so there's no record on your phone of where you went, then go here, and clear your browsing history.

History   ⓘ Q ✕

Your Google Account may have other forms of browsing history at myactivity.google.com.

CLEAR BROWSING DATA...

If you want to erase more than just websites (passwords, for example) then go to "Settings" at the very bottom of the menu. This opens up more advance settings.

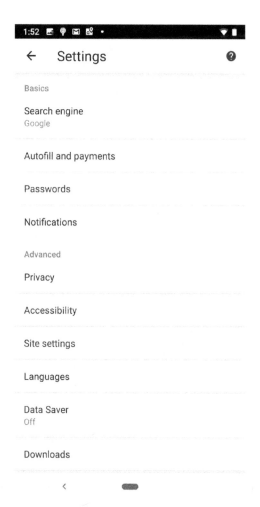

[6]

SNAP IT!

This chapter will cover:
- How to take different photos
- How to take videos
- Camera settings
- Different camera features

The camera is the bread and butter of the Pixel phone. Many people consider the Pixel to be the greatest camera ever on a phone. I'll leave that for you to decide.

One of the nice things about photos on the Pixel is it stores them online automatically, so you don't have to worry about losing them. You can see them by logging into the Google account associated with your Pixel and going here:

https://photos.google.com

Best of all: this is all free! You don't have to pay extra for more storage and it doesn't go against other things in your Google Drive.

To make sure you have this feature on, go to "Settings" and "Backup" and "sync"; make sure you toggle it on.

There are some caveats (such as the photos may be compressed), so read the terms.

THE BASICS

Are you ready to get your Ansel Adams on? Let's get started by opening the Camera app. You can do this several ways:

- The most obvious is to tap the Camera on your favorite bar or by swiping up and opening it from all apps. It looks like a camera—go figure!

Camera

- Double press the power button.

Once you are in the app, don't forget, you can twist the phone to toggle between selfie mode.

When you open the app, it starts in the basic camera mode. The UI can look pretty simple, but don't be fooled. There are a lot of controls.

The first is at the top. Tap the down arrow at the top of the screen.

The options are pretty straightforward, but "Top Shot" (which used to be called Motion) might be new to you. This is basically like a very short video of your photo. You can turn it on for all photos, auto so it turns on when motion is detected, or turn it off. Top Shot is larger, so storing it in this mode will take a little more space. Night Sight is ideal for when you in low light. The screen below is the basic camera settings, but this menu can differ slightly depending on what camera mode you are in.

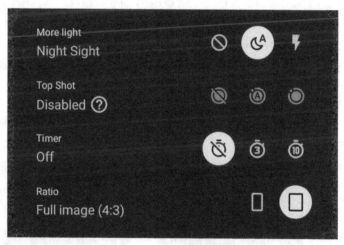

Over on the upper right side is the folder icon; that lets you pick where you will save the photo you are currently shooting.

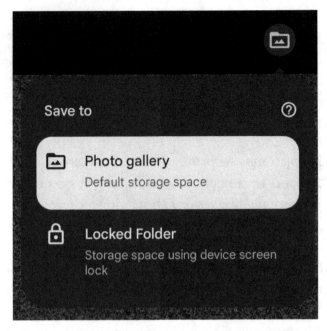

On the bottom of the screen are all the modes and the shutter. Starting with the top row from the left you have the selfie button, the shutter, and the last photo preview (tapping that will show all of your photos that you have taken starting with the most recent). On the bottom, you have the camera modes, which I'll cover in more detail later in this chapter.

When you point your camera at a product and tap and hold over that product, this will activate Google Lens, which will try to detect what you are pointing at and give you more information about it. It's not always 100% accurate (for example, I pointed it at the Pixel 5 case and it showed me info for the Pixel 3), but it's still a nice feature.

If you tap once, but don't hold, this will bring up exposure and zoom options (you can also pinch in and out to zoom). Tapping on the area of the screen that you want to focus on will also focus on that area; for example, if you point it at a group of people in front of a crowd of people, you can tap the group to tell the camera that's the focus of the show.

When you tap in the middle of the screen as you prepare to take a shot, you can use the sliders to control the amount of brightness, contrast or warmth the photo has.

One final thing I will point out about taking pictures. Remember up in the top bar (when you swipe down), there's an option to disable the camera or mic? Well you sort of need those things to take photos and videos, right? If you try and do it when they're on, you'll get the message below. Tap the unlock button to enable the features.

HELLO (PHOTO) FRIEND

Do you have people you take photos of more than others? A kid? A partner? A friend? A pet? Google's AI can prioritize people you photograph most. To turn it on go to the Camera app, open the settings and enable Frequent Faces.

CAMERA MODES

Let's look at each of the modes next.

Think of modes like different lenses. You have your basic camera lens, but then you can also have a lens for fisheye, and close up. If you look at the bottom of your camera app, you can slide left and right to get to the different modes. In 2019, Google added Night Sight mode, which helps you capture better photos at night. It works like the basic Camera mode. It also turns on automatically when it detects you are shooting in night.

Next to Night Sight is Portrait mode. Portrait mode gives your photos a sharp professional look to them. It blurs the background to really make your photos pop. I'll show an example with a photo of myself—apologies in advance for my looks!

Here I am with zero blur:

And here I am with maximum blur:

So how do you do that? First, slide to the Portrait mode. The phone will try to figure out where the focal point will be, but you'll get the best effect if you tap on the screen where the focus will be. If you tap on the face, for example, it will tell the phone you want to blur everything else. The change won't be noticeable—you can edit it after.

I'll show you how to edit that blur a little later in this section.

Video mode takes, you guessed it, videos! Once you tap record, there are not as many settings as the camera. To the left, there's a pause button, the middle is the stop button, and the far right is the camera shutter—that means as you are recording you can still take photos.

When you tap to focus on a subject, you'll notice that there's only a slider for zoom (bottom), and brightness (right side); there's also a lock to lock in on your focus.

There's also a Cinematic video mode that takes videos with the blurred effected—only the main person in the scene is in focus.

Before you shoot a video, there's also an option to toggle between Slow Motion, Normal, and Time Lapse; if you are coming to the Pixel 5 from an earlier model, you'll probably be used to using these modes in another place; they used to be located under "More." Google decided to eliminate that extra step and put all the video modes in one place.

So speaking of this "More" area, let's tap on that next and see the other modes available. There's three more:

Panorama, Photo Sphere, and Lens. The modes can take good photos, but they are more fun modes.

Panorama is great for landscape photos. The below photo is an example (note: this was not shot on the Pixel):

The way it works on the Pixel, is you take one photo, and then you move a little to the right and take another, and so on and so forth; then all of those photos are stitched together to make one giant photo. Just hit the arrow button for each photo and the blue button to finish (or X button to cancel).

Photo Sphere is sort of like a panorama photo; it's several photos stitched together. But where a panorama is straight, Photo Sphere is 360 degrees; it's fun for your phone or sharing online (like Facebook). To use it, tap the shutter when in Photo Sphere mode, then move your camera up and down, and left and right.

Before you take the photo, you can also tap the down arrow at the top of the screen and change the shape.

When you view the photo, you can either use your finger to move the direction of it, or you can tap the VR mode in the lower right corner and use VR headsets.

The last mode is Lens. I already mentioned how you can activate it in the regular camera mode, but there are more features in the native Lens mode.

You can do automatic, but there are modes within this mode to translate, scan a doc, look for consumer products, or identify food. By default, it's on the automatic mode (the middle one), but tapping on the other icons will switch the mode and give you more accurate results.

Most modes have unique settings. Translate, for example, lets you auto-detect the language you are scanning, or change it to something different.

Depending on what you scan, it will give you information about the product, and you can click for more information.

EDITING PHOTO
=============

EDITING PHOTO

Editing photos is one of the many places that Good really shines. This is where AI really takes over—you can remove people from photos, move them to different places, change their expressions, and even change a bright sunny day into something dreary.

You can access editing by opening the photo you want to make edits to. This is done by either opening it from the camera app by clicking on the photo preview (next to the shutter);

Or by opening the Photo app.

When you open a photo, the first thing you'll want to do is tap the Edit button.

The top row is your menu options. Below the options, you'll see all the menus. The first thing that comes up is always Suggestions; this is always dynamic. It changes based on how the AI thinks it can make the photo better. Sometimes it's spot on. Sometimes...not so much.

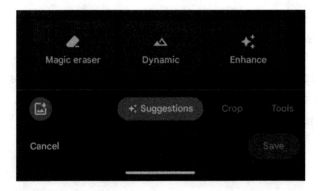

Magic Editor

One of the big features of Pixel is the Magic Editor. This uses AI to let you make huge tweaks to a photo—for example, you can move someone standing on a beach but not by the water, to the waters edge.

It's AI and sometimes works better than others. You'll probably notice in some photos edges and other markings that make it clear that the photo is not 100% real. It really depends on the photo.

You also might not see the option right away; if you have a brand new phone, make sure you do all the updates—both phone updates and app updates.

So let's try it out. To get started tap the Magic Edit button in the lower left side of the screen.

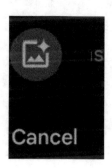

It will take a few seconds to load, so be patient. For this example, I'm going to take an old wedding photo—yes, you can make edits to older photo (in the example below, the photo is 15 years old); I'm going to move myself from the left side of the bench to the right side.

The first thing I'll do is circle what I want to move—it doesn't have to be precise.

After a few seconds, you'll see a white shadow around what Google thinks you want to move.

You can now drag the portion of the image wherever you want it to go.

As you drag it, you can also pinch outward to make the image bigger or smaller.

When you are satisfied with where the image is going to be placed, let go and tap the checkmark in the lower right corner. The image will start regenerating. It will take a few seconds.

When it's done, it will have several photos to toggle through, and you can pick the best one. You can see in the image below that it's not perfect; in my example, a shadow has been left where I was previously seated. If you aren't happy, try again—circling something else—or try another photo.

SKY TOOL

Another feature promoted is the ability to change the sky in a photo. It's not quite night and day, but it still is pretty cool.

If you go to Tools on a photo with a background that's outdoor, you should see the Sky option. Tap that. In my example, I'm going to change a very bright sky to something more dreary.

It's not a drastic change, but you can see how it does look more overcast now.

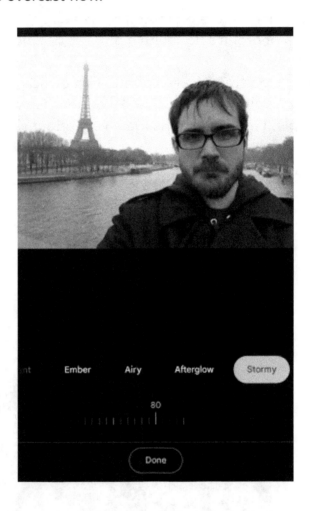

The tools menu also gives you the option to apply a blur effect to a photo. So I can put the focus on me and not that structure in the background.

And, I'll point out again, this is an older photo—it was taken over ten years ago on an iPhone. I say that to make it clear that you can use whatever photo—shot from whatever device—that you want.

MAGIC ERASER

Tools also has one of the newest and most exciting features: Magic Erase. Want to erase the photobomber from the image? Done! That old high school sweetheart who broke your heart? Gone!

Before talking more about this magic eraser tool, let me briefly mention that if you are editing a portrait photo, you'll see even more options (see image below).

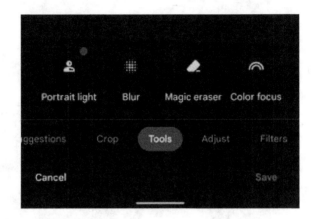

This is where you can change the focus of the image (so you can blur something else), adjust the lighting, or reduce the amount of blur.

But back to that core feature: magic erase. How does it work? Let's take a look. The image below is great, isn't it?! But I don't like that statue on the left.

To remove her, I go into Edit > Tools, select Magic eraser.

From here, I just rub my finger on the area that I want to erase.

When I'm done, I lift my finger. Poof. She's all gone!

Pretty cool, right? Make sure and tap Done and save it.

If by chance you don't see this feature, then you probably need to update your phone. Also, remember, this feature is currently only available on the Pixel.

OTHER ADJUSTMENTS

Next to Tools is the Adjust button. This is where you can manually adjust things like brightness. Suggestions will also do this, but it will do it automatically.

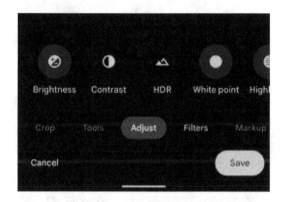

Clicking on any of the settings will bring up a new slighter; move it left or right to adjust the intensity.

Filters is the next setting, and it will automatically apply a filter over the photo. So if you want it to have a Vivid look—i.e. one that's full of bright colors, then tap the Vivid filter.

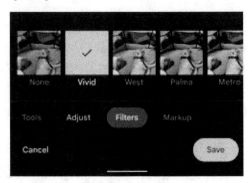

The last setting is Markup. This setting is used to write text or highlight things in the photo. For example, if you want to circle something in the photo that you are trying to point out to someone.

BLURRED PHOTOS

Google's AI really helps photos shine. The unblur feature shows you the full potential of this AI engine; it can take previously blurry photos and sharpen them.

It's under Tools and says Unblur. Tap that once, and it will automatically make the adjustment that it thinks is appropriate for the photo.

Once the adjustment is made, you'll see a slider that lets you make more adjustments—100 is the max you can go; going down would in values would make the photo more blurry.

ORGANIZING YOUR PHOTOS

The great thing about mobile photos is you always have a camera ready to capture memorable events; the bad thing about mobile photos is you always have a camera ready to capture events, and you'll find you have hundreds and hundreds of photos very quickly.

Fortunately, Google makes it very simple to organize your photos so you can find what you are looking for.

Let's open up the Photos app and see how to get things organized.

Photos

Pixel keeps things pretty simple by having only four options on the bottom of your screen.

In the upper right corner, there's three dots, which is the photo option menu; that menu is there no matter where you are in the Photo app.

When you tap that menu, you'll get several more options.

The options are as follows:
- Select – This lets you select photos on your screen so you can share, email, print, and more.
- Layout – There are two Layout modes: Comfortable view (this view creates a grid with small and large photo thumbnails) and Month view (all thumbnails are the same size.

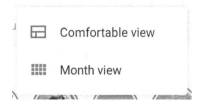

- Album – Let's you create an album by selecting photos or faces.

✕   Select faces
Photos of selected faces will be shared

- Shared album – Lets you share albums.
- Prints – Quickly create photo albums that you can print and have sent to your house.

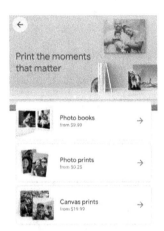

- Movie – Movies lets you create video memories of your photos. You can either select "New movie" and create one based on selected photos or pick from one of the many templates. It can take several minutes for movies to generate when you pick this option.

- Animation – Animation is kind of like a .gif; whereas movies could run for several minutes, animations are only a few seconds.
- Collage – Collage lets you pick up to nine photos to combine into one collage. If you pick less, Google will automatically arrange it for you. The below is an example of three photos in a collage. There isn't a lot of customization here, so if you want a collage, you might want to download a free collage app that has a few more tools in it.

In the upper left corner is three lines; this opens your second menu option screen.

Some of the options (such as buy prints) are the same ones you've already seen in the other menu.

Photo frames is an option available if you have a Google Nest Hub (or Google Hub). This lets you pick the photos that display on your Hub.

← Photo frames

Get started with your first photo frame. Once set up,
you can manage the albums it displays here.

Google Nest Hub

Relive your favorite memories. See your
best shots from Google Photos appear
automatically from your phone to your home.

$129*   Buy

*Terms apply.

Device folders is where you can find screenshots if you've taken any. You can take a screenshot by pressing the orange button and the down volume button at the same time.

Archive is to help you declutter your phone. You can archive photos so your main photo area has less photos; archiving them puts them here, but they will still be searchable.

Clear the clutter

Archived items will be kept here. They'll still
show in albums & search results.

Learn More

If you delete a photo, it is actually not permanently deleted from your device...yet. It is moved here. This is helpful if you have a kid who likes to delete things! If you tap any of the photos, you can restore it or delete it— deleting it means it's gone for good.

"Free up space" removes photos from your device and backs them up to your Google account. You can still view them whenever you want.

Settings will be covered in the next sections.

Finally, PhotoScan is a free app that you have to download to use; the app lets you use your Pixel camera to scan old print photos. It works surprisingly well and is recommended if you have lots of photos that you want saved.

The next tab on the bottom of the Photos app (Albums) is where you can go to start grouping your photos together. There are already things like Places and Things that have albums; if you have starred anything, you'll also see one for Favorites.

What you might not know is Google is quietly working in the background to figure out who is in photos. Once you take several photos, you'll see one called People & Pets.

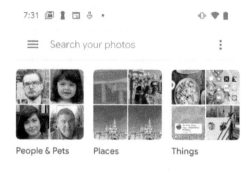

When you open it, you'll see people you probably recognize, and when you click on it, it will show you other photos that they are in. Pretty cool, right? What's cooler is you can name those people, so you can search more easily for them. Just click their face, then tap "Add a name." In the example below, Google has found my dog's face.

I added her name, so when I go back, I now see her photo with her name. I can now search for photos using her name. You can also search for photos using names of places or even foods or things. The photo search is pretty smart, and it gets even smarter as you take more photos.

When you want to create a new album, just click the three dots in the upper right corner.

It will ask you to name it; you can pick whatever you want. From here, you can either auto select things based on people and pets, or you can select your own photos.

If you select photos on your own, you'll just have to manually tap each one that you want in the album.

If you select to have it auto create, you'll just have to pick what you want to use (a person's name, for example).

Once the album is created, you can tap the three dots in the upper right corner to add more photos, order photos, delete the album, or share.

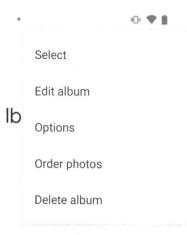

You can also click the Share button on the album (or on any photo), which brings up the Sharing menu. You can share with a link, via email, Bluetooth, text message, and more.

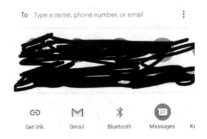

The Assistant option is recommendations from Google's AI bot; it collects memories based on places you've been and groups together what it considers the best shots.

The last option on the bottom menu is Sharing. Sharing lets you select other people who can see your photos. You can, for example, share all photos of a certain person with that person, and you can set it to share new photos of that person whenever you take them.

To get started, just tap the "Add partner account."

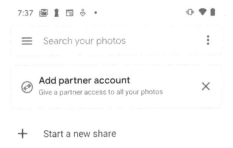

Next you'll see a screen telling you what sharing is. Tap the blue "Get Started" option.

Share your library

1 Select your partner

2 Choose what you want to share

Get Started

Learn more

From here you'll search for the person's name or email; Google might also have a few suggested contacts for you, and you can just tap their name.

To   Type a name or email   ⋮

SUGGESTIONS

Once you pick the person, it will ask you what you want to share. You can share every single photo now, and in the future, or you can pick certain people or days.

← **Choose Settings**   Next
Share with diana.lacounte@gmail.com

GRANT ACCESS TO

All photos   ◉

Photos of specific people   ○

OLDER PHOTOS

Only show photos since this day
Off

It will confirm what you are sharing before it shares; once you tap "Send invitation," it will email an invite to that person and they have to accept it before they actually see the photos.

SETTINGS

You probably won't spend a lot of time in Photo settings, but they're still good to know for those occasions when you do want to make changes.

You can access your settings by opening the Photo app, tapping on the three lines in the upper left corner, then tapping on Settings.

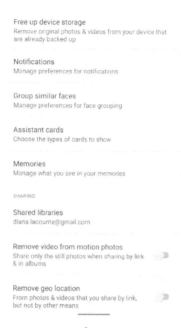

There are three areas of the settings: Main, Sharing, and Google apps.

MAIN SETTINGS

- Back up & sync – Lets you pick how photos are backed up (what email account they are linked to, the resolution of the photos, when to back them up, where to back them up, and more).
- Free up device storage – Removes photos from your device and stores them in your account so you have more room for additional photos.
- Notifications – Lets you pick the kinds of pop up notifications you'll receive regarding photos (suggested sharing, printing promotions, photo book drafts, suggested photo books).
- Group similar faces – Turn on and off face grouping; if you don't want a robot scanning

your photos to figure out the person that's in the shot, you can disable it here.

- Assistant cards – Picks the cards that show up in the Assistant menu of the Photos app (Creations, Rediscover this day, Recent highlights, Suggested Rotations, Suggested Archive).
- Memories – Memories are usually fun; seeing Google show you a photo of your kid as a baby can put a smile on your face as you start your day. But sometimes memories can suck—you go through a messy divorce or a loved one dies, and Google is there to remind you of their face. You can take those people out of your memories here. It doesn't delete them from your account; you just won't see them show up in your feed.

SHARING SETTINGS

- Shared libraries – Lets you see who can view your photos.
- Remove video from motion photos – Motion photos are nice—they're also big. If you prefer to just show the photo and not the video clip that goes with it, you can turn it off here.
- Remove geo location – Your photos have geo tags on them (unless you turn them off); that means when you share a photo, it might have things like your home address. If you don't want people to see that, then you can disable geo location with the people you are sharing it with.

GOOGLE APPS

- Google Location settings – Lets you pick what apps can see your photos.
- Google Lens – Not a setting as much as instructions about how to use the app.

[7]

GOING BEYOND

This chapter will cover:
- System settings

If you want to take total control of your Pixel, then you need to know where the system settings are and what can and can't be changed there.

First the easy part: the system settings are located with the rest of your apps. Swipe up, and scroll down to "Settings."

Settings

There's a lot of settings here. Below are the available ones:

- Network & Internet
- Connected devices
- Apps
- Notification
- Battery
- Storage
- Sound & Vibration
- Display
- Wallpaper & Style
- Accessibility
- Privacy
- Location
- Safety & emergency
- Security
- Passwords & Accounts
- Digital Wellbeing & parental control
- Google
- System
- About phone
- Tips & support

I'll cover what each setting does in this chapter.

NETWORK & INTERNET

This setting, like most settings, does exactly what it sounds like: connects to the Internet. If you need to connect to a new wireless connection (or disconnect from one) you can do it here. Tapping on the current wireless lets you see other networks, and the toggle lets you switch it on and off.

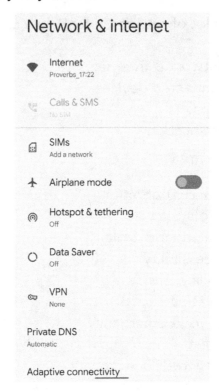

Mobile network is for your carrier (Verizon, AT&T, Sprint, etc.).

Data usage tells you how much data you've used; tapping on it gives you a deeper overview, so you can see exactly which apps used the data. Why is this important? For most, it probably won't be. I'll give an example of when it helped me: I work on the go a lot; I use the wireless on my phone to connect my laptop (which is called tethering); my MacBook was set to back-up to the cloud, and little did I know it was doing this while connecting to my phone...20GB later, I was able to pinpoint what happened by looking at the data.

Below this is Hotspot & tethering. This is when you use your phone's data to connect other devices; you can use your phone's data plan, for example, to use the Internet on your iPad. Some carriers charge extra for this—mine (AT&T) includes it in the plan. To use it, tap the setting and turn it on, then name your network and password. From your other device, you find the network you set up, and connect.

Airplane mode is next. This setting turns off all wireless activity with a switch. So if your flying and they tell you to turn everything wireless of, you can do it with a switch.

Finally, Advanced is for doing some wireless connecting on a private network. This is not something a beginning user would need to do, and I'm not going to cover it, as the point of this book is to keep it ridiculously simple.

CONNECTED DEVICES

"Connected devices" is Google's way of saying Bluetooth. If you have something that connects via Bluetooth (such as a car radio or headphones) then tap "Pair new device." If you've previously paired something, then it will show below and you can simply tap it to reconnect.

APPS

Every app you download has different settings and permissions. A map app, for example, needs your permission to know your location. You can turn these permissions on and off here. Does it really matter? App makers can't abuse it, right? Sort of. Here's an example: a few months ago, a popular ride-sharing app made headlines because it wanted to know where passengers were after they left the ride, so they could promote different restaurants and stores and make even more money. Many felt this was both greedy and an invasion of privacy; if you are of the latter stance, then you could go in here and stop sharing your location.

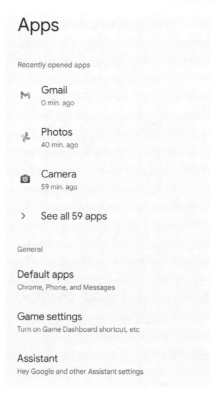

You can also use this setting to turn on Game Short-cuts.

NOTIFICATIONS

Want to see the notifications you accidently dismissed? You can find that in the Notifications settings. You can also decide the priority people get when you get notifications. Bubbles let's conversations come in like floating icons; you can turn that on and off here.

Notifications

Manage

App settings
Control notifications from individual apps

Notification history
Show recent and snoozed notifications

Conversation

Conversations
No priority conversations

Bubbles
On / Conversations can appear as floating icons

Privacy

Device & app notifications
Control which apps and devices can read notifications

Notifications on lock screen
Show conversations, default, and silent

BATTERY

The battery setting is more about analytics than settings you can change. There are some settings here you can edit—you can put your phone in battery saving mode, for example. This setting is more useful if your battery is draining too quickly; it helps you troubleshoot what's going on so you can get more life from your phone.

A SMARTER BATTERY

Google's AI can extend into your battery life. By default, the Pixel automatically will go into Battery Saver mode when you get to 10% battery remaining. That's great. But you can also set it to go on based on your routine. So Google's AI predicts your daily habits and adjust the battery accordingly.

To use this mode, go to the System Settings app, then tap Battery and Battery Saver. Next tap Set a Schedule. Tap the option that says "Based on your routine."

STORAGE

The Pixel has no expandable storage for SD; that means whatever you buy for your phone, that's the amount you have. You can't upgrade it later.

When you first get your phone, storage won't be a big issue, but once you start taking photos (which are larger than you think) and installing apps, it's going to go very quickly.

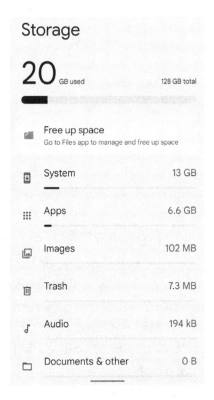

The storage setting helps you manage this. It shows you what's taking up storage, so you can decide if you want to delete things. Just tap on any of the subsections and follow the instructions for what to do to save space.

SOUND & VIBRATION

There's a volume button on the side of your phone, so why would you need to open up a setting for it?! This setting lets you get more specific about your volume.

For example, you may want your alarm to ring super loud in the morning, but you want your music to play very low.

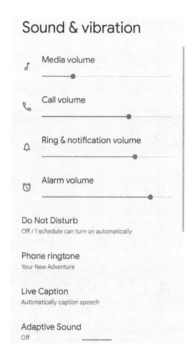

Sound & vibration

Media volume

Call volume

Ring & notification volume

Alarm volume

Do Not Disturb
Off / 1 schedule can turn on automatically

Phone ringtone
Your New Adventure

Live Caption
Automatically caption speech

Adaptive Sound
Off

DISPLAY

As with most of the settings, almost all the main features of the Display setting can be changed outside of the app. If you tap "Advanced," however, you'll see some settings not in other places. These include changing colors and font sizes.

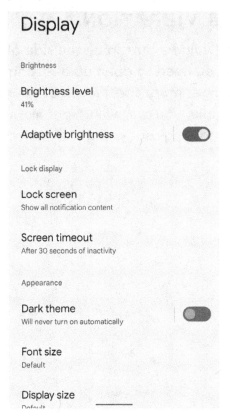

WALLPAPER & STYLE

This setting is nothing more than the setting that comes when you access wallpaper from your homescreen.

Wallpaper & style

Change wallpaper

Wallpaper colors   Basic colors

ACCESSIBILITY

Do you hate phones because the text is too small, the colors are all wrong, you can't hear anything? Or something else? That's where accessibility can help. This is where you make changes to the device to make it easier on your eyes or ears.

PRIVACY

Like Location Control (covered below), Privacy settings got a big upgrade in Android 12. It's so big, it now fills an entire section in the settings.

Go to System > Privacy and tap "Advanced" to see all of them.

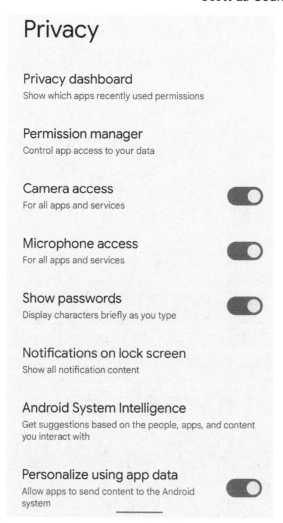

The biggest upgrade is the ability to customize what apps see what; it's no longer all or nothing. You can refine exactly how much or how little each app can see.

The Privacy Dashboard is one of the easiest ways to see what apps are doing. In the example below, it shows in the past 24 hours, most my apps were using my location.

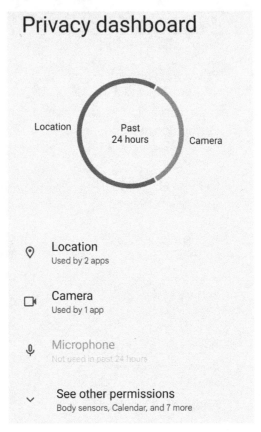

Tapping on Location will reveal what apps were using the location.

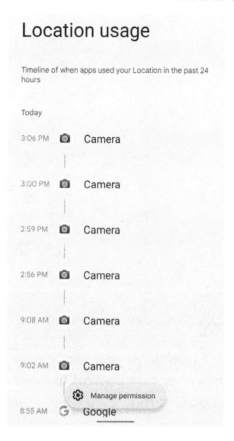

You can then tap on Manage permissions (either on this screen or the main settings screen) to disable location sharing.

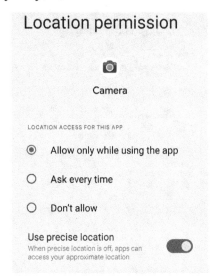

SECURITY

If you want to change your lock screen, add an additional fingerprint, or turn on / off the find your phone setting, you can do it here.

LOCATION

In the past, Location Control was an all or nothing feature—you'd decide if an app could see you all the time or none of the time. That's nice for privacy, but not nice for when you actually need someone to know your location— like when you are getting picked up by a ride app like Lyft. The new Android OS adds a new option for while you are using the app. So, for example, a ride app can only see your location while you are using the app; once the ride is over, they can no longer see what you are doing.

To pick what location an app can see, go to System > Location and select the app, then tap when they can see your location.

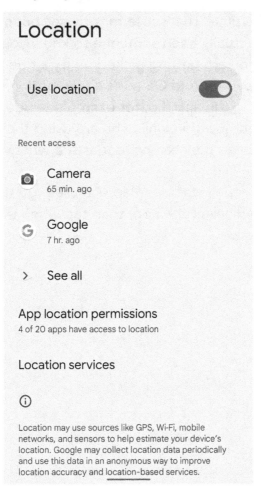

SAFETY & EMERGENCY

These settings let you add important details about you —like your blood type; they also let you enable safety features—like crash detection if your mobile device detects a motion that is common with car accidents.

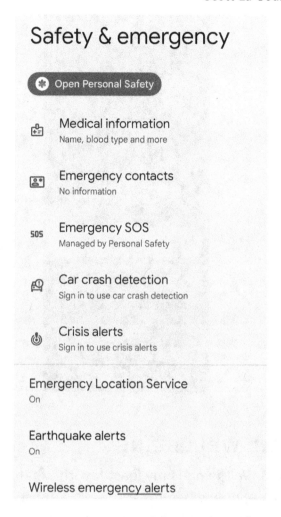

CAR CRASH DETECTION

Nobody hopes to use this feature, but you'll be thankful for it if the unthinkable happens. With crash detection turned on, your phone will alert emergency services if it detects you have been in a car accident. It won't call immediately, it will give you a prompt to tell you what it's doing, so if it's a mistake, you can stop it. To turn it on, go to Settings > Safety & emergency > Car crash detection.

DIGITAL WELLBEING

Digital Wellbeing is my least favorite feature on the Pixel phone; now when my wife says "You spend too much time on your phone"—she can actually prove it!

The purpose of the setting is to help you manage your time more. It lets you know your spending 12 hours a day updating your social media with memes of cats, and "hopefully" make you feel like perhaps you shouldn't do that.

Digital Wellbeing & parental controls

ılı Your Digital Wellbeing tools

Use app timers and other tools to keep track of screen time and unplug more easily

Show your data

👥 Parental controls

Add content restrictions and set other limits to help your child balance their screen time

GOOGLE

Google is where you will go to manage any Google device connected with your phone. If you are using a Google watch, for example; or a Chromecast.

SYSTEM

System is important for one very important reason: system updates. If you don't have your phone set to download updates automatically, then you'll have to do it manually here.

Tap the "Advanced" button.

This gives you a menu with more features. One is the "System update." If there's an update available, it will say it. If it says it, then tap it.

 System update
Update available

You'll have to restart your phone before it downloads.

Security update available

This update fixes critical bugs and improves the performance and stability of your Pixel 3. If you download updates over the cellular network or while roaming, additional charges may apply.

Update size: 108.5 MB

   Restart now

You can also change the language in this setting as well as make changes to gestures and put limits on users.

ABOUT PHONE

This is where you will find general information about your phone. Such as the OS you are running, the kind of phone you have, IP address, etc. It's more of an FYI, but there are a few settings here that you can change.

TIPS & SUPPORT

This isn't really a setting. It's just tips and support. You can also talk with support here.

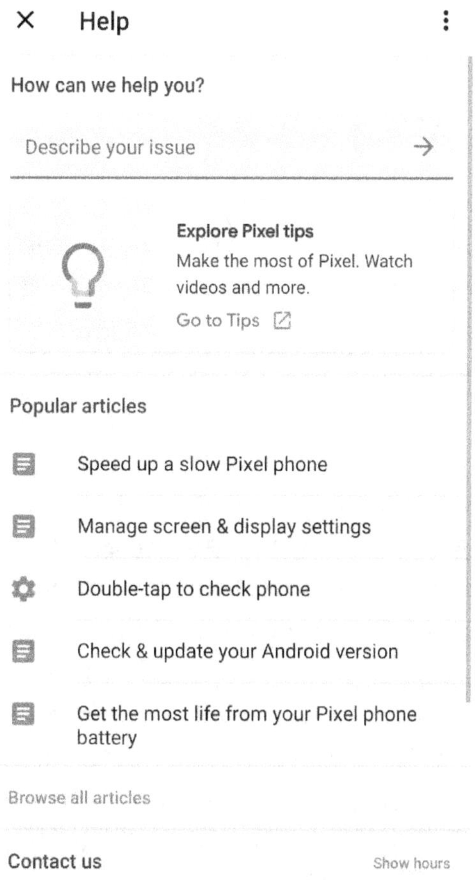

✕   Help   ⋮

How can we help you?

Describe your issue   →

Explore Pixel tips
Make the most of Pixel. Watch
videos and more.
Go to Tips ⬀

Popular articles

▤   Speed up a slow Pixel phone

▤   Manage screen & display settings

⚙   Double-tap to check phone

▤   Check & update your Android version

▤   Get the most life from your Pixel phone
    battery

Browse all articles

Contact us   Show hours

CONCLUSION

Congratulations on completing your journey through this comprehensive guide! We've covered a lot of ground, from the basics of navigating the Google Pixel 8a's interface to mastering its powerful features.

It's worth acknowledging that technology evolves rapidly, and new updates may introduce changes to the device's functionality. Therefore, continuous learning will keep you abreast of all the enhancements and improvements that will undoubtedly come to the Google Pixel 8a.

Remember, the key to mastering any piece of technology is practice and exploration. The more you experiment with your Pixel 8a, the more you'll discover its potential. Don't be afraid to delve into the settings, adjust preferences, and try new apps. The beauty of such a powerful and versatile device like the Pixel 8a is that it can adapt to suit your needs, and it's capable of so much more than you might initially realize.

I hope this book has equipped you with the knowledge and confidence to fully harness the power of your Google Pixel 8a. Here's to many hours of productive, fun, and transformative experiences with your new device. Enjoy the journey!

BONUS BOOK: MASTERING GOOGLE SEARCH

GOOGLE SEARCH PRO TIPS

This chapter will cover:
- What is a Boolean search?
- Google Search Operators
- Basic commands

THE MATH OF SEARCHING

History lesson time: becoming a Google search expert owes a lot of credit to math. If you are like me—someone who needs a calculator for simple addition—then you are probably thinking, "Oh, no! Time to close this book and forget I ever thought about becoming better at Google search!"

Don't worry! You'll be fine! It owes a lot to math, but it doesn't look like the kind of math that you ran from in high school.

The math we are talking about is Boolean algebra. Basically, it's the kind of problems with true / false statements.

When you are using Boolean in traditional math it can get a little complicated; in a search, not so much. A typical Boolean search is going to look a little like this:

Boolean AND search

What's the purpose of this kind of search? Precision. It makes it easier to find what you want without combing through lots of webpages.

There are three main types of Boolean searches: AND, NOT, and OR.

You probably already guessed what they do. AND searches both terms, which Google already does.

NOT excludes terms. For example, let's say you want to search for administrator jobs that aren't related to being a manager. You could search for:

Administrator NOT manager

OR searches for either or. For example:

Computer OR pc

Not exactly the math you are used to, right?

GOOGLE SEARCH OPERATORS

Google has a whole set of commands that go beyond the typical Boolean ones above (which you can also use). They call these Google Search Operators.

There are dozens of "operators"—Google frequently adds more (and takes away others); so, if something in this book doesn't work, make sure you have read it right, but remember there is a chance that Google took it out.

As an example, a few years back, you could use this to find phone numbers:

Phonebook:john doe

This is no longer the case.

One search operator that's been around for years is the calculator. Google "calculator" and you'll see a working calculator appear in your search. That's pretty cool, right? What's cooler is you can just search for equations.

For example, I'll type in 60*8 (the * means times—FYI, the divide sign looks like this /):

You can make your calculations pretty complex; for example, here's what (60*8)/(12)+8 looks like:

Google's search calculator can do more than basic math. You can search for conversions, too. It's helpful for cooking and pretty much everything else.

Here's how it would look if you wanted to know what 100 feet is in inches:

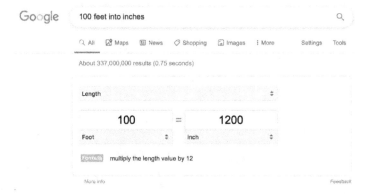

Remember: this stuff works on the mobile version of search as well. So, let's say you are travelling and need to know how much something is in USD—just search for it. Here's an example of a search for 200 yen to usd:

COMMON GOOGLE SEARCH OPERATORS

As I've already mentioned, there are dozens of operators, but this section will cover the most common you will use.

Price

If you are hunting for a product, then search for it with a price value. For example, let's say you want a Chromebook, and your budget is $200. Search "Chromebook $200" and you'll get results like this:

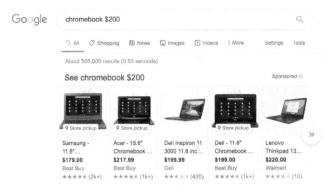

The above search will give you a pretty broad range of computers. If you know your budget, then you can search for that as well. Let's say your budget is $200 to $250 for that Chromebook. That search would look like this:

Chromebook $200...$250

Exclude Words

Sometimes you search for things that have more than one meaning. As an example, think about the word "Bronco." There's the Ford Bronco truck, but also a horse named the bronco and a football team. What if you want to know the speed of a bronco, but you are referring to the horse, not the truck? Use the minus (-) key:

Bronco speed -truck

Exact Matches

When you search for words in Google, it's looking for the term—but also looking for pages that have each of the words. If you only want to find the exact term, then you can add quotes. For example, instead of searching broadly for:

Tallest man

You can use quotes: "Tallest man." In the first example, it's looking for webpages that contain both tallest and man in any combination. In the second, it's only looking for that exact phrase.

You can also combine search with the Boolean searches above (e.g. AND, OR, NOT). For example:

"Tallest man" AND "United States"

Excluding Words and Wildcards

If there are words you absolutely do not want, then you can use the minus (-) key. If there's a term you want either, but not necessarily both, of the words (for example it can be a webpage with Disneyland or Theme park) then you can do a wildcard search with the * key (e.g. "Disneyland * Theme park").

Site Search

Google can do more than search millions of pages—it also can search just one page. What I mean by that is you can do a Google search on a specific domain. Just put "Site:" in your search and the domain you are searching for. For example, let's say I wanted to find out about the literature programs at Cal State Fullerton University. I can use this search term to do that:

Site:Fullerton.edu literature

Google   site:fullerton.edu literature   Q

Q All   Images   News   Books   Videos   More   Settings   Tools

About 5,720 results (0.34 seconds)

Annotated Bibliographies & Literature Reviews - Literacy and Re...
https://libraryguides.fullerton.edu › ... › Literacy and Reading Education
Aug 20, 2019 - Literacy and Reading Education: Annotated Bibliographies & Literature
Reviews. This research guide was created to support students in the ...

Major in Comparative Literature - Department of English, Compar...
english.fullerton.edu › academics › comp_major ▾
The Bachelor of Arts in Comparative Literature emphasizes the comparative study of literatures
across the globe. The comparative literature major trains ...

Related Search

Have you ever read a news website or visited an ecommerce store and wanted to see similar websites? Related search lets you do that. Simply add "Related:" and the domain you want to see similar websites to into your search bar. For example, if I wanted to see websites that are similar to Amazon.com, I would Google this:

Related:amazon.com

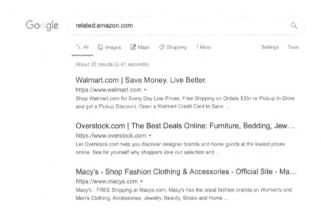

MORE GOOGLE SEARCH OPERATORS

The next operators are useful, but not as commonly used.

Around Search

Some of these searches get a little complicated. An around search is one such search. The search looks for terms close together. Let's say you are looking up a politician's stance on immigration. You want to search for the politician's name mentioned around the word immigration, specifying how many words should separate them. For example, if I want to find "Biden" within six words of "immigration," I would search for this:

Biden AROUND(6) immigration

That tells Google to make sure the two terms are only six words apart or less. If "Biden" appears in the first paragraph, and "immigration" appears several paragraphs down, then it wouldn't come up as a result.

Definitions

Is there a word you don't know and want the definition? Don't go to your dictionary! Just Google "Define:" and you'll get the definition at the top of your results. Such as:

Define: onomatopoeia

Cache

A cache search is something commonly used for marketers doing SEO reviews, but not so much for everyday searchers. It shows you the page that Google has most recently crawled (which means the last time a bot went to the page to see if it had been updated). To perform the search just type in "Cache:" and the website. For example (make sure you don't leave a space):

Cache:whitehouse.gov

Filetype

If you are looking for a document—not a website—a file search will help you out. Let's say it's tax season and you need your 1099. You don't want to go to the instructional website that tells you about the form. You just want the form. Try this search:

1099 filetype:PDF

Notice how all the results have a PDF in them?

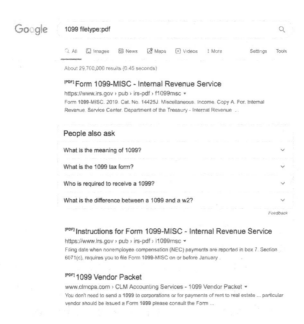

This also works for other file types (DOCX, TXT, PPT, and more—if you don't see the filetype there, then experiment because it may have been added by the time of this writing).

Group Items

If you have multiple terms you want to group together, then you can use "( )". For example, let's say you are interested in two products from the same company; you could use a term like this:

(switch OR 3ds) Nintendo

Map
If you want a map of a city, just search for "Map:" and the name of the city. For example:

Map: Anaheim

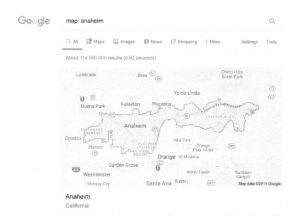

If you need a map of a specific address, just type in the address (no need to add "map" to the search). You'll get a zoomed-in view (sometimes it will have a street view as well), and in the lower right corner, there's an option for directions.

Movie Showtimes

Heading to the movies? Google "Movie:" and the name of the movie to get the latest showtimes. For example:

Movie: Spider Man Far From Home

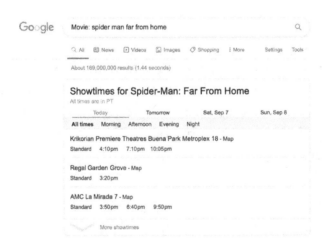

Notice how it doesn't ask for locations? That's because it knows my location based on my IP. That's kind of convenient, but what if I'm going to another location to see the movie? Just add a location to the end. For example:

Movie: Spider Man Far From Home New York City

Source Search

Later in this book, I'll talk about different places to search (image search, news search, video search, etc). This search query applies to news search, which you can perform at google.com/news. If you want to see only a specific newspaper, magazine, or blog, then search "Source:" and the name of the publication. For example:

Source: New York Times

Stock Search

If you are a financial buff, you can search for ticker information (such as current price) by typing "Stock:" and the ticker symbol (some companies will still come up if you type the company name and not the symbol, but the symbol is always the best practice). For example:

Stock:dis

You also have the option to follow the stock by clicking on the blue button in the upper right corner.

Title Search

Something that's helpful when looking for news articles is an Intitle search. It finds websites, too. What the search does is looks for the term in the page title. For example:

Intitle:Microsoft

You can search for multiple terms in the title with "Allintitle" For example:

Allintitle:Microsoft surface

You can also search for terms in the text (not title) with "Intext" and "Allintext."

URL Search

Very similar to the Intitle search is the Inurl search. Where the Intitle search searches the page title, the Inurl searches URLs. So, if you are looking for websites that have Paleo in the URL, then search for this:

Inurl:paleo

Just as you can search for all terms with "Allintitle," you can search for all terms in URL with "Allinurl." For example:

Allinurl:paleo recipes

Weather

Forget the weather apps or going to webpages for the weather, just type in "Weather:" and the city to your search and get the forecast in your results. For example:

Weather:Kabul

SEARCHING BEYOND WEBPAGES

This chapter will cover:
* Searching for books
* Searching for finance
* Searching for flights
* Searching for images
* Searching for maps
* Searching for news
* Searching for products
* Searching for videos
* Searching for you!

BEYOND GOOGLING

If you've ever "Google'd" something, then you probably started with google.com. That's a great place to start...for some keywords. But Google has evolved over the years and created more than just a web search engine.

If you are searching for images, for example, then you can use an entirely different search engine.

The operators I showed you in the first chapter will largely apply to these searches as well—it's a bit hit or miss, so some will work better than others.

Some are more complicated than others. I'll cover each one here. As with all things in this book, remember that Google takes things out and adds things in regularly, so if you don't see it, then chances are they've removed it.

You can see all the different types of searches you can perform when you do a regular Google search. Notice all the options below the search? Including one that says more?

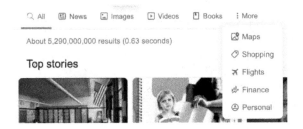

SEARCHING FOR BOOKS

The first option I'll cover is books. You can find it here:

Google.com/books

As you might have guessed, it searches for books. At first glance, it looks pretty simple. It's just a search bar. (If you've downloaded books from the Google Play store, those will show up on a bookshelf below that.)

You may be thinking, "Nice…but I find my books at Amazon or Barnes & Noble."

I don't blame you for thinking that. Those are both great places to buy books. Google, however, is a great place to find books, too. Why? Because the filters are more advanced. They've also worked with a lot of universities to digitalize collections, so you can find electronic copies of books and search inside them—sometimes they're even free. A lot of these books are rare and out of print.

On the right corner of the search, there's a config button. When you click on that, there's an option for "Advanced Book Search."

The advanced search gives you over a dozen options to narrow your search.

For this book, I'll do a very basic search for "Hurricanes."

Once the results come back, I can start filtering them. I can show, for example, all books, or only books with previews, or only books that are free.

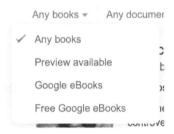

Next to "Any books" I can search for the type of document I'm looking for (e.g. any, books, magazines, newspapers).

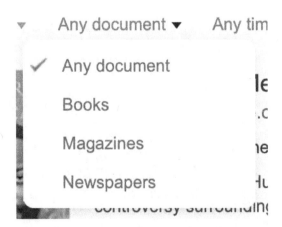

Finally, I can search for when it was published. This is especially useful if you have a specific range or are looking for a rare book—for example, you want to read what people were saying about the flu in 1751.

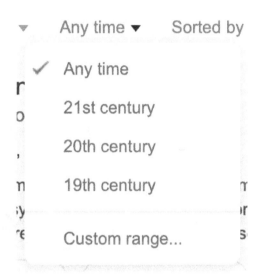

SEARCHING FOR FINANCE

The finance search is a bit like having a financial newspaper in the cloud—except you make it more personal. To get to it, go to:

Google.com/finance

The first thing you'll see is a dashboard with all the markets—and, if you follow any, companies you follow.

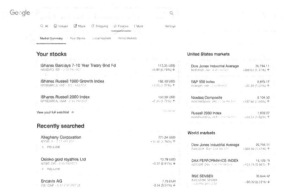

If you scroll down on the page, you'll see local market news.

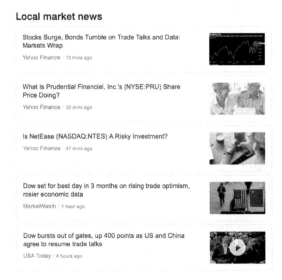

And further down, world market news.

World market news

European shares close mostly higher with the exception of the UK FTSE

Forexlive · 2 hours ago

Why Gold is a better hedge for the GBP than the FTSE 100

Forexlive · 12 hours ago

S&P 500, FTSE 100 Futures Up as U.S.-China to Hold Trade Talks

Yahoo Finance · 14 hours ago

S&P 500, FTSE 100 Futures Up as U.S.-China to Hold Trade Talks

Bloomberg · 15 hours ago

Thyssenkrupp to leave Germany's blue chip index DAX, MTU Aero joins

Reuters · 22 hours ago

More world market news →

Up top—right under the search box—there are four different options for different markets.

Market Summary   Your Stocks   Local Markets   World Markets

The search itself is pretty basic. You search for companies. Instead of a traditional search where you get webpages, however, it shows you the current state of the stock. There's also a follow button in blue if you want to add the company to your finance dashboard.

Below the stock information, you can get all the company news.

And below the news, you can grab the company's quarterly financial report.

Quarterly financials

(USD)	Jun 2019	Y/Y
Revenue	20.25B	32.94% ↑
Net income	1.76B	39.64% ↓
Diluted EPS	0.97	50.26% ↓
Net profit margin	8.69%	54.62% ↓

More financials →

Disclaimer

SEARCHING FOR TRAVEL

Expedia, Priceline, and similar travel sites are great, but Google takes it up a notch with more filtering and integration with their own services (such as Google Maps). When you use their search, you are usually booking through the actual airline or hotel, with Google managing things on the backend. It's just as secure as any other travel website.

To check out how it works go to:

Google.com/flights

As the URL implies, flights are what the search is known for, and they are the first thing you see. But there's more here, as you'll quickly learn.

When you search for your trip, you can do all the standard filters you can do pretty much anywhere else—make it one way, add passengers, and switch from economy to business or first class.

As you search for the dates, you can also see about how much it will cost—this is helpful if your dates are flexible as it helps you find the cheapest time to travel.

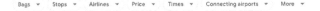

After you search for the flight, you can begin filtering by price, how many stops, and more.

You can also track the price to see if it goes up or down over time.

If you want to see how much it is on different dates, those options are shown again; in addition, you can see how much the flight is at a nearby airport—sometimes rates are cheaper if you go to a smaller airport.

When you are ready to book, you'll have the option once more to pick the fare that you want—economy, first class, etc.

On the left side, there's a menu with several other options. Let's look at hotels next.

One of the first things you'll notice when you do a hotel search is there's an option to look for both hotels and vacation rentals.

To make sure you are getting what you want, you can filter by reviews.

You can filter by the amenities they offer.

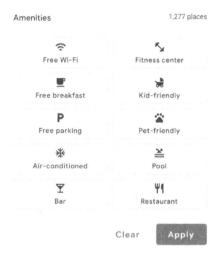

And you can search only for certain companies (e.g. Hilton, Marriot, etc).

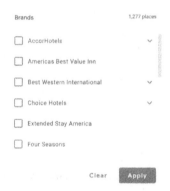

There are also options to filter by the hotel class.

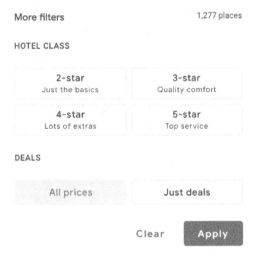

Finally, you have the option to filter by a specific price point / range.

The map on the right side shows you where different hotels are located, which is helpful if you will be seeing people nearby.

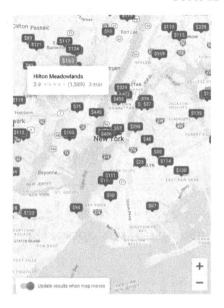

If you want to bundle your flight and hotel together—which usually gives you a slightly discounted rate—then click the "Packages" option on the left menu.

One of my favorite features about this Google search is the menu option labelled "Explore." This helps you see all the popular sites and attractions for the city.

If you click "Day plans" on the top, it will give you sample itineraries (note: this option is not available for all cities).

As an example, I clicked on "If you only have a day" and it gave me a list of what to see and a map of how to do it. Each step tells me how long it will take by car (subway is also available, depending on the city and where it's located in the city).

Right above the location, if I click how long it takes by car, it will take me to a map with driving directions.

Up on the top of this map is a list of all the different ways you can get there (subway, bike, walking, etc). Some will obviously be greyed out as you can't fly to the locations. The direction times will change based on what you pick—and, in the case of walking, it will take you down one-way streets.

SEARCHING FOR IMAGES

Google Images is a powerful tool if you are looking for images to stick into presentations, term papers, or anything else.

It's always important to remember that images can have copyrights, so make sure you understand the terms before using one publicly.

To get started with an image search, go here:

Google.com/images

It looks much like a normal Google search at first. Type in what you want a picture of and search away.

The biggest difference is the camera button next to the magnifying glass. Click that and you can search by an image's URL, or you can upload the image. Uploading an image is especially useful if you want to see if other people are using your work without your permission.

For this book, I'm going to search for puppies because who doesn't love puppies?

Some searches have smarter results than others. In this case, it tells me different breeds I can search for. You won't always see those suggestions.

Over in the upper right corner, there's a drop box that says, "Filter explicit results." Because this is an image search, this makes sure nothing inappropriate slips through. Use it or don't use it, but know that Google doesn't censor, so sometimes things come up that you may not expect to see.

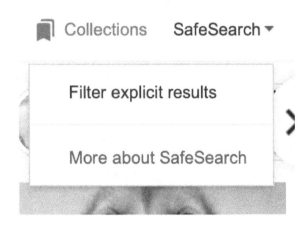

Near the right side, there's an option that says "Tools." When you click that, you'll see all the different filters.

The filters are largely self-explanatory. Size lets you show only photos that are a certain size—if you want a wallpaper for your computer, for example, you would select large.

Color lets you look for full color, black and white, transparent, or a certain shade. Transparent means the background is clear, FYI.

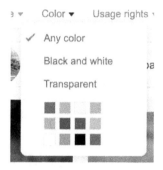

Usage rights can help you find photos you can reuse without permission. Be careful here! Just because it says it's fine, doesn't necessarily mean it is. It could be misclassified, someone else could have put it up without the person's permission, or a number of other things. If you are using a photo you found on a Google Image search commercially, then do so at your own risk.

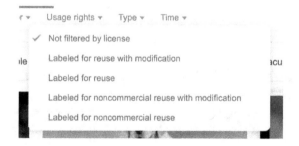

Type lets you pick the file type—if you are searching for an animated GIF for an email, for example.

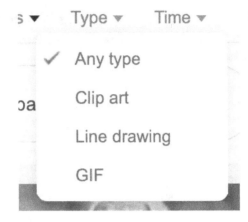

Time is when the photo was added.

When you click the image, you get a preview on the right side.

You also have the option to share or bookmark it.

If you click on the image, it opens to the webpage containing the image.

If you only want to open the image, then go back to your results, right click the image, and click "Open image in new tab."

That opens the page with only the image.

SEARCHING FOR MAPS

Google Maps is probably something you've used before. It comes up whenever you do normal searches for restaurants and businesses. But you can also search there directly here:

Google.com/maps

The common story you should notice by now is it's a very simple user interface.

The top left corner is where you do your searching. Before you search, however, you can also browse. So, for example, let's say you are looking for something to eat in your area. Just click the restaurant button.

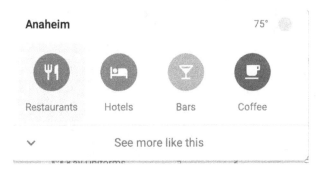

If you don't see what you want, click "See more like this" and then select the grey "More" button, which brings down several other options.

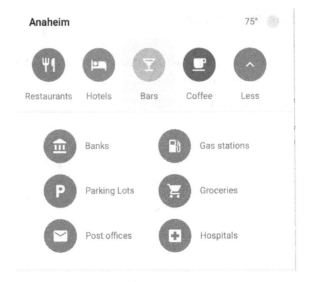

Once you click what you want (I'm using "Restaurants" in this example) you'll get a list of the results with reviews. Clicking on any of them will show you where it's at on the map; it will also show you the hours, website (if available), photos, and more.

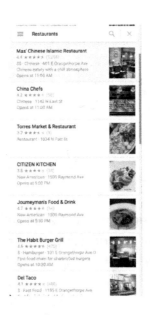

When you click "Restaurants," you can also go back to that search and click at the end of the word. This will bring up an autocomplete that asks you if you want to see only nearby restaurants.

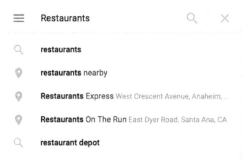

You can filter your results by price, ratings, hours, and type of cuisine.

On the lower right side, you can use the little yellow man to get a street view of your location.

Drag him wherever you want to see on the map.

That will bring up a street view of the location.

SEARCHING FOR NEWS

If you are a news junky and want to search for news stories, head over to:

Google.com/news

While the news search is pretty cool, it's not the re-search tool you are hoping for if you are serious about finding information. Many sources here will show you the current news, but make you pay for older news. If you need to find older stories, visit your local library—most libraries subscribe to news databases that are free to use; many of these can be used at home if you have a library card from that library.

The news section on the left side lets you sort your news by subject.

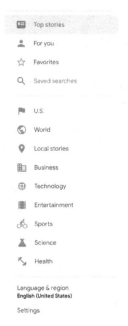

When you search for news, you can click the little arrow on the right side of the search bar to bring down a more advanced search. Here you can search for phrases and dates.

SEARCHING FOR PRODUCTS

Google isn't exactly known for shopping, but it's definitely worth checking out. You can see it here:

Google.com/shopping

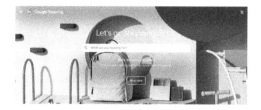

You can either search or browse for products.

When you search for products, there are a lot of filters on the left menu that you can apply.

One of the more helpful ones is "available nearby" which helps you find stores in the area that sell the product.

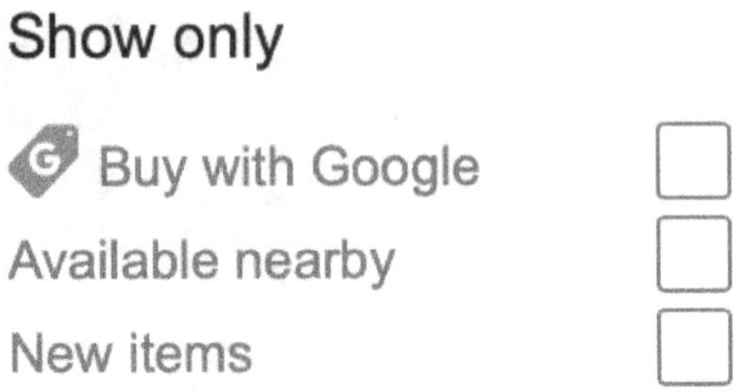

Show only

Buy with Google

Available nearby

New items

You can also shop by price point.

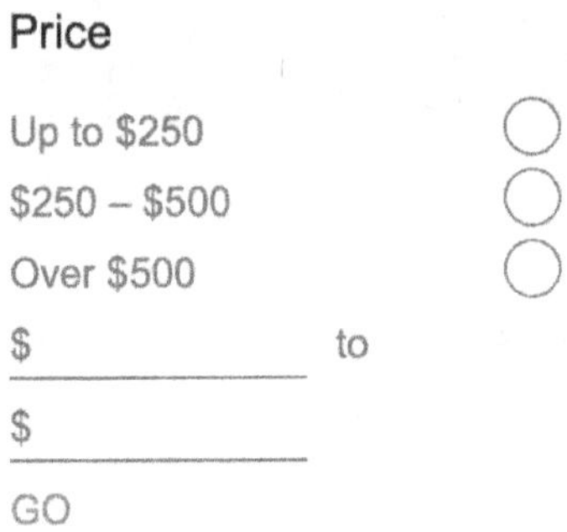

Price

Up to $250

$250 – $500

Over $500

$ _____ to

$ _____

GO

Depending on what you are searching for, there will be several unique filters. In the example below I searched "iPhone," and Google then let me filter by things like battery life.

Battery Life

10 – 14 hours ○

14 – 21 hours ○

Over 21 hours ○

By default, you'll get your results in a list, but clicking on the grid button in the right corner switches the layout.

In the upper left corner is the button to bring up settings.

This lets you see your orders, saved searches, and more.

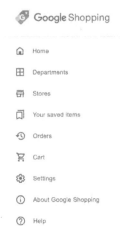

SEARCHING FOR VIDEOS

Google owns YouTube and it makes sense that you would search for videos there. Using the search engine at the below link, however, will search for videos on YouTube and beyond:

Google.com/videohp

The search looks almost identical to the main Google search.

The results page, however, is a little bit different.

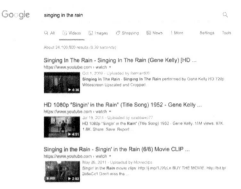

When you click tools on the right side (below the magnifying glass) you'll get expanded filters that you can apply (it's very similar to how image searching works).

You can search by duration, which is helpful if you are looking for a full movie and not just a clip.

When it was uploaded.

If you want it in any quality or if it has to be HD.

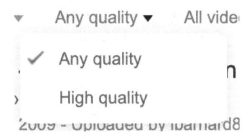

If you only want videos with closed captioning.

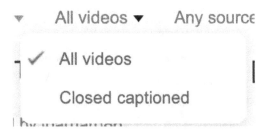

And finally, if you want to see a specific source that the video is coming from.

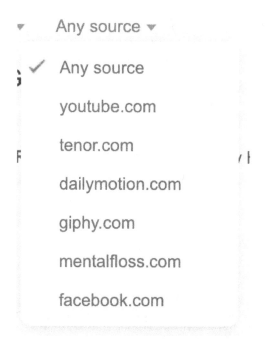

Many of the matches in the results also let you see similar videos. Look for the drop-down arrow next to the link if it applies.

SEARCHING FOR YOU!

The Google Personal Search is something Google has added and dropped and added again—so there's a chance it could be dropped again in the future.

A Google Personal Search looks through your personal files for matches—things like email and photos. It's all private, so even though it kind of looks like a Google search results page, nobody but you can see it.

Unlike other searches that have a dedicated domain, the easiest place to start a personal search is at google.-com. Just type in what you are looking for.

When the results come back, click the "More" button and select "Personal."

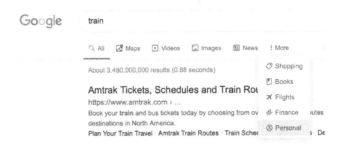

You can use the Google Personal Search to find photos.

Your photos
Only you can see these results

Emails.

Gmail
Only you can see these results

And the websites you have been browsing.

Your browsing history
Only you can see these results

INDEX

ABOUT THE AUTHOR

Scott La Counte is a librarian and writer. His first book, *Queit, Please: Dispatches from a Public Librarian* (Da Capo 2008) was the editor's choice for the Chicago Tribune and a Discovery title for the Los Angeles Times; in 2011, he published the YA book The N00b Warriors, which became a #1 Amazon bestseller; his most recent book is   *Consider the Ostrich.*

He has written dozens of best-selling how-to guides on tech products.

You can connect with him at ScottDouglas.org.

www.ingramcontent.com/pod-product-compliance
Lightning Source LLC
LaVergne TN
LVHW051321050326
832903LV00031B/3289